AN INVESTOR'S GUIDE TO TRADING OPTIONS

*T*he Options Industry Council (OIC) is pleased to introduce *An Investor's Guide to Trading Options*, a primer on options investing. The guide clarifies options basics, explains the options marketplace, and describes a range of strategies for trading options.

An Investor's Guide helps fulfill OIC's ongoing mission to educate the investing public and the brokers who serve them about the benefits and risks of exchange listed options. We believe that education is the key to sound and intelligent options investing, and that the tremendous growth of the options market in recent years can be attributed, at least in part, to the value of this education.

Formed in 1992 by the nation's options exchanges and The Options Clearing Corporation, OIC is your options education resource. We are always available to answer your questions and to expand your options knowledge. To contact OIC, please visit our website at www.888options.com or phone our call center at 1-888-OPTIONS.

The Options Industry Council

LIGHTBULB

PRESS

D0171922

The information in this guide is provided for educational purposes. Neither The Options Industry Council (OIC) nor Lightbulb Press is an investment adviser and none of the information herein should be interpreted as advice.

For purposes of illustration, commission and transaction costs, tax considerations, and the costs involved in margin accounts have been omitted from the examples in this book. These factors will affect a strategy's potential outcome, so always check with your broker and/or tax adviser before engaging in options transactions.

The options strategies described in this book are possibilities, not recommendations. No strategy is a guaranteed success, and you are responsible for doing adequate research and making your own investment choices. Please note: All equity options examples represent a standard contract size of 100 shares.

Options are not suitable for all investors. Individuals should not enter into option transactions until they have read and understood the risk disclosure document *Characteristics and Risks of Standardized Options*. Copies of this document may be obtained from your broker, from any exchange on which options are traded, or by contacting The Options Clearing Corporation, One North Wacker Dr., Suite 500 Chicago, IL 60606 (888-678-4667). It must be noted that, despite the efforts of each exchange to provide liquid markets, under certain conditions it may be difficult or impossible to liquidate an option position. Please refer to the disclosure document for further discussion on this matter.

LIGHTBULB PRESS
Project Team

Design Director Dave Wilder
Designer Kara W. Hatch
Editorial Staff Joan Kim, Mavis Morris, Kristin Szostek
Production and Illustration Mercedes Feliciano, Katharina Menner, Tina Sbrigato, Matthew Smith, Thomas F. Trojan

SPECIAL THANKS TO
Gary Kreissman at GKL Media; Debbie Baratz, Dan Busby, Jean Cawley, Joe Harwood, Cheryl Jurich, Carolyn Mitchell, Bill Ryan, and Pamela Tvrdy at The Options Clearing Corporation; Kathy Simmons at the International Securities Exchange; the American Stock Exchange; the Chicago Board Options Exchange; the International Securities Exchange; the Pacific Exchange; the Philadelphia Stock Exchange; and The Options Clearing Corporation.

ARTWORK CREDITS
The AMEX logo is used with the permission of the American Stock Exchange. The CBOE logo provided as a courtesy by Chicago Board Options Exchange, Incorporated, and LEAPS® is a registered trademark of CBOE. The ISE logo is used with the permission of the International Securities Exchange. The PCX logo is used with the permission of the Pacific Exchange. The PHLX logo is used with the permission of the Philadelphia Stock Exchange. The image on page 30 ©2003 Lightbulb Press and its licensors. All rights reserved.

CONTENTS

AN INVESTOR'S GUIDE TO TRADING OPTIONS

THE BASICS

INVESTING STRATEGIES

RESEARCH AND INFORMATION

GLOSSARY AND INDEX

What Is an Option?

An option is a contract to buy or sell a specific financial product officially known as the option's underlying instrument or underlying interest. For equity options, the underlying instrument is a stock, exchange-traded fund (ETF), or similar product. The contract itself is very precise. It establishes a specific price, called the **strike price**, at which the contract may be **exercised**, or acted on. And it has an **expiration date**. When an option expires, it no longer has value and no longer exists.

Options come in two varieties, **calls** and **puts**, and you can buy or sell either type. You make those choices—whether to buy or sell and whether to choose a call or a put—based on what you want to achieve as an options investor.

BUYING AND SELLING

If you buy a call, you have the right to buy the underlying instrument at the strike price on or before the expiration date. If you buy a put, you have the right to sell the underlying instrument on or before expiration. In either case, as the option holder, you also have the right to sell the option to another buyer during its term or to let it expire worthless.

The situation is different if you **write**, or sell, an option, since selling obligates you to fulfill your side of the contract if the holder wishes to exercise. If you sell a call, you're obligated to sell the underlying interest at the strike price, if you're assigned. If you sell a put, you're obligated to buy the underlying interest, if assigned.

As a writer, you have no control over whether or not a contract is exercised, and you need to recognize that exercise is always possible at any time until the expiration date. But just as the buyer can sell an option back into the market rather than exercising it, as a writer you can purchase an offsetting contract and end your obligation to meet the terms of the contract.

TYPES OF OPTIONS CONTRACTS

Calls

BUY
The right to buy

SELL
The obligation to sell

AT A PREMIUM

When you buy an option, the purchase price is called the **premium**. If you sell, the premium is the amount you receive. The premium isn't fixed and changes constantly—so the premium you pay today is likely to be higher or lower than the premium yesterday or tomorrow. What those changing prices reflect is the give and take between what buyers are willing to pay and what sellers are willing to accept for the option. The point at which there's agreement becomes the price for that transaction, and then the process begins again.

If you buy options, you start out with what's known as a **net debit**. That means you've spent money you might never recover if you don't sell your option at a profit or exercise it. And if you do make money on a transaction, you must subtract the cost of the premium from any income you realize to find your net profit. As a seller, on the other hand, you begin with a **net credit** because you collect the

WHAT'S A FINANCIAL PRODUCT?

The word *product* is more likely to conjure up images of vegetables or running shoes than stocks or stock indexes. Similarly, *instrument* might suggest a trombone or a scalpel rather than a debt security or a currency. But both terms are used to refer to the broad range of investment vehicles.

An options contract gives the buyer rights and commits the seller to an obligation.

Puts

BUY
The right to sell

HOLDER

SELL
The obligation to buy

WRITER

premium. If the option is never exercised, you keep the money. If the option is exercised, you still get to keep the premium, but are obligated to buy or sell the underlying stock if you're assigned.

THE VALUE OF OPTIONS

What a particular options contract is worth to a buyer or seller is measured by how likely it is to meet their expectations. In the language of options, that's determined by whether or not the option is, or is likely to be, in-the-money or out-of-the-money at expiration. A call option is in-the-money if the current market value of the underlying stock is above the exercise price of the option, and out-of-the-money if the stock is below the exercise price. A put option is in-the-money if the current market value of the underlying stock is below the exercise price and out-of-the-money if it is above it. If an option is not in-the-money at expiration, the option is assumed to be worthless.

An option's premium has two parts: an intrinsic value and a time value. Intrinsic value is the amount by which the option is in-the-money. Time value is the difference between whatever the intrinsic value is and what the premium is. The longer the amount of time for market conditions to work to your benefit, the greater the time value.

Finding values	For example
Share market price	$25
– Exercise price	– $20
= **Intrinsic value**	= $ 5
Premium	$ 6
– Intrinsic value	– $ 5
= **Time value**	= $ 1

OPTIONS PRICES

Several factors, including supply and demand in the market where the option is traded, affect the price of an option, as is the case with an individual stock. What's happening in the overall investment markets and the economy at large are two of the broad influences. The identity of the underlying instrument, how it traditionally behaves, and what it is doing at the moment are more specific ones. Its volatility is also an important factor, as investors attempt to gauge how likely it is that an option will move in-the-money.

OLD AND NEW

American-style options can be exercised any time up until expiration while European-style options can be exercised only at the expiration date. Both styles are traded on US exchanges. All equity options are American style.

How Does Options Trading Work?

You should know whether you're opening or closing, buying or purchasing, writing or selling.

BUYER   **SELLER**

Options trading can seem complicated, in part because it relies on a certain terminology and system of standardization. But there's an established process that works smoothly anytime a trade is initiated.

OPEN AND CLOSE

When you buy or write a new contract, you're establishing an **open** position. That means that you've created one side of a contract and will be matched anonymously with a buyer or seller on the other side of the transaction. If you already hold an option or have written one, but want to get out of the contract, you can **close** your position, which means either selling the same option you bought, or buying the same option contract you sold.

There are some other options terms to know:

- An options **buyer** purchases a contract to open or close a position

- An options **holder** buys a contract to open a **long position**

- An options **seller** sells a contract to open or to close a position

- An options **writer** sells a contract to open a **short position**

All options transactions, whether opening or closing, must go through a brokerage firm, so you'll incur transaction fees and commissions. It's important to account for the impact of these charges when calculating the potential profit or loss of an options strategy.

STANDARDIZED TERMS

Every option contract is defined by certain **terms**, or characteristics. Most listed options' terms are standardized, so that options that are listed on one or more exchanges are **fungible**, or interchangeable. The standardized terms include:

Contract size: For equity options, the amount of underlying interest is generally set at 100 shares of stock.

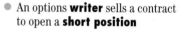

Expiration month: Every option has a predetermined expiration and last trading date.

Exercise price: The available strike prices for an option may be one, two and a half, five, or ten point increments that bracket the current market price of the underlying equity. The increment that's used depends on the market price of the equity.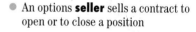

Type of delivery: Most equity options are **physical delivery** contracts, which means that shares of stock must change hands at the time of exercise. Most index options are **cash settled**, which means the in-the-money holder receives a certain amount of cash upon exercise.

Style: Options that can be exercised at any point before expiration are American style. Options that can be exercised only on the day of expiration are European style.

Adjustment provisions: Representatives from each exchange determine any

L E A P S®

EXPIRATION

LEAPS®
Long-Term Equity AnticiPation Securities®, or **LEAPS**,
are an important part of the options market. Standard options have expiration dates up to one year away. LEAPS, however, have expiration dates up to three years away. LEAPS are traded just like regular options, and each exchange decides the securities on which to list LEAPS, depending on the amount of market interest. About 10% of all listed options are LEAPS.

LEAPS allow investors more flexibility, since there is much more time for the option to move in-the-money. At any given time, you can buy LEAPS that expire in the January that is two years away or the January that is three years away. Once expiration is a year away, LEAPS are converted to standard options.

EXERCISE AND ASSIGNMENT
Every option that expires in a given month usually expires on the Saturday after the third Friday of the month. That means the last day to trade expiring equity options is the third Friday of the month. If you plan on exercising your options, be sure to check with your brokerage firm about its cut-off times. Firms may establish early deadlines to allow themselves enough time to process exercise orders.

When you notify your brokerage firm that you'd like to exercise your option:

adjustments that might be made to the terms of an options series in response to a stock split, merger, or other corporate action.

An **options class** refers to all the calls or all the puts on a given underlying security. Within a class of options, contracts share some of the same terms, such as contract size and exercise style. An **options series** is all contracts that have identical terms, including expiration

QUADRUPLE WITCHING DAY
In the last month of each quarter—on the third Friday of March, June, September, and December—the markets typically experience high trading volume due to the simultaneous expiration of stock options, stock index options, stock index futures, and single stock futures. This day is known as **quadruple witching day**—up one witch since the introduction of single stock futures.

1 Your brokerage firm ensures the exercise notice is sent to The Options Clearing Corporation (OCC), the official guarantor of all listed options contracts.

2 OCC assigns fulfillment of your contract to one of its member firms that has a writer of the series of option you hold.

3 If the brokerage firm has more than one eligible writer, the firm allocates the assignment using an exchange-approved method.

4 The writer who is assigned must deliver or receive shares of the underlying instrument—or cash, if it is a cash-settled option.

CASHING OUT
Some options are subject to automatic exercise, which means that if they are in-the-money by specified amounts at expiration OCC automatically exercises the option on behalf of the holder, unless instructed otherwise. Individual brokerage firms often have their own policies too, and might automatically exercise any options that are in-the-money by a certain amount. You should check with your brokerage firm to learn whether automatic exercise applies to any of your long positions.

month and strike price. For example, all LMN calls are part of the same class, while all LMN February 90 calls are part of the same series.

Options Class   Options Series

On Which Securities Are Options Offered?

You can buy or sell options on stocks, indexes, and an orchestra's worth of other instruments.

In 1973, the first year that options were listed, investors could write or purchase calls on 16 different stocks. Puts weren't available until 1977. Today the field of option choices has widened considerably—in 2003, investors could buy or write calls and puts on over 2,300 different stocks and stock indexes.

ADR

Single Equity

The most common options, and the ones that individual investors are most likely to trade, are those on specific equities, typically the stocks of large, widely held companies. It's generally quite easy to find current information about those companies, making it possible for investors to make informed decisions about how the price of the underlying stock is likely to perform over a period of months—something that's essential to options investing. These options may also be multiply listed, or traded on more than one exchange.

TO LIST OR NOT TO LIST

Options aren't listed on every stock, and each exchange doesn't list every available option. **The Securities and Exchange Commission (SEC)** regulates the standards for the options selection process, and beyond that, exchanges can make independent decisions. There are some rules, though.

On every options exchange, a stock on which options are offered must:

- Be listed on the NYSE, AMEX, or Nasdaq National Market for at least three months

- Have a minimum of 2,000 shareholders and seven million outstanding shares

- Have a specified minimum average trading price during an established period of time

In addition to those minimum qualifications, stocks are chosen based on the stock's volatility and volume of trading, the company's history and management, and perceived demand for options. This subjective component to the decision-making process explains in part why some exchanges may choose to list an option while others do not.

In general, options are available on the most well-known, publicly traded companies, since those are the stocks that are most likely to interest options investors. A company is not responsible for options listed on its stock, though some exchanges require the com-

It's important to understand the difference between equity options and employee stock options. Unlike listed options, which are standardized contracts, employee stock options are individual arrangements between an employer and an employee. Usually, stock options grant the employee the right to purchase that company's shares at a predetermined price after a certain date. Employee stock options cannot be traded on the secondary market. Employers usually grant stock options as part of compensation packages, hoping to provide an incentive for employees to work hard, since they'll share in any success of the company—to the extent that success is expressed in a higher stock price.

EQUITY OPTIONS

STOCK OPTIONS

Foreign Currency

Stock Index

INDEXING THE MARKET

Index options, which were introduced in 1983, are also popular with individual investors. The underlying instrument is a stock index instead of a single equity. Because they track the prices of many stocks, indexes can reveal a movement trend for broad or narrow sectors of the stock market. The S&P 500 index tracks 500 large-cap US stocks, for example, while the Dow Jones Utility Average, an index of 15 utility companies, is used to gauge the strength or weakness in that industry.

Unlike options on stock, index options are cash settled, which means that upon exercise, the writer is obligated to give the holder a certain amount of cash. The total settlement is usually $100 times the amount the option is in-the-money.

A 90 call on the DJIA at 9300	3
	x $ 100
DJX is 93	**You receive $300**

For example, if you exercised a 90 call on the DJIA when the index is at 9300 and DJX is at 93, you'd receive $300 (or 3 x $100), before fees and commission. Index options can be more expensive than stock options, but they may offer more leverage and less volatility.

An index reflects changes in a specific financial market, in a number of related markets, or in an economy as a whole. Each index—and there are a large number of them—measures a market, sector of the market, or economy. Each is tracked from a specific starting point, which might be as recent as the previous trading day or many years in the past.

pany's consent before listing the option. Most companies welcome the listing of options on their stock, since historically a stock's trading volume tends to rise after a new options class is issued on that stock.

OFF THE LIST

It's possible for exchanges to decide to delist options, or remove them from the trading market. If the trading volume for an option remains low for a long period of time, an exchange may decide that a lack of investor interest in that option makes it not worth listing. In addition, exchanges must delist options if they fail to meet certain criteria.

In general, options that have already been listed on a particular stock at the time that option is delisted may be traded until they expire. No new expiration months will be added on that class.

OTHER OPTIONS

While the most popular options are those offered on individual stocks, exchange-traded funds (ETFs), and stock indexes, contracts are also available on limited partnership interests, American Depository Receipts (ADRs), American Depository Shares (ADSs), government debt securities, and foreign currencies. Many debt security and currency options transactions are initiated by institutional investors, such as banks.

GROWTH SPURT

The total number of options trades that takes place each year has grown dramatically, just as the variety of available options has grown. On the first day of trading, there were 911 transactions on the 16 listed securities. Today, an average daily volume might be close to one million on a single exchange.

In 1973, the first year of listed options trading, 1.1 million contracts changed hands. In 2003, the year's total volume was more than 800 million contracts on the five exchanges.

Where Are Options Traded?
Options transactions take place on exchanges through open outcry or electronic matching.

If you've been trading stocks for some time, you're already familiar with the basic procedures that govern options trading.

Individual investors who wish to buy or sell options place orders through their brokerage firms. Where an order goes from that point depends on both the brokerage firm's policy and the exchange or exchanges on which the options contract is traded.

AMERICAN STOCK EXCHANGE®

INTERNATIONAL SECURITIES EXCHANGE.

CBOE
CHICAGO BOARD OPTIONS EXCHANGE

A JOB FOR A SPECIALIST

Traders acting as specialists lead the auctions for each options class, and are in charge of maintaining a fair and orderly market, which means that contracts are easily obtainable, and every investor has access to the best possible market price.

Each exchange has a particular structure of specialists, who may sometimes be known as designated primary market makers (DPMs), lead market makers (LMMs), competitive market makers (CMMs), or primary market makers (PMMs). Other traders, sometimes known as agents, trade all types of options for their clients, sometimes buying from and selling to the specialists.

ELECTRONIC TRADING

New technology has supplemented or replaced the traditional open outcry system on some exchanges. Instead of traders gathering in a pit or on a floor, transactions are executed electronically, with no physical interaction between traders. Auction prices are tracked and listed on computers, and orders may be filled within a matter of seconds.

Some options exchanges are totally electronic, and many use a hybrid of open outcry and electronic trading. The majority of the orders that come to those exchanges are filled by an automatic execution computer that matches the request with a buyer or seller at the current market price. Transactions requesting an **away-from-the-market price**, or one that is higher or lower than the current market price, are held in an electronic limit order book. Once trading reaches the requested price, those customers' orders in the book are the first to be handled.

Proponents of electronic trading argue that the anonymous nature of the transactions means that all customers—whether represented by an experienced broker or not—have equal footing, which makes the market fairer. They also point out that since the costs of running an electronic exchange are lower, the transaction fees for trades may also be lower.

BUY

STANDARD OF EXCHANGE

Listed options are traded on **regulated exchanges**. The Securities and Exchange Commission (SEC) regulates the exchanges, and all of them must adhere to rules designed to make trading fair for all investors. The oldest is the Chicago Board Options Exchange, or CBOE. Options are also traded on the American Stock Exchange (AMEX), the International Securities Exchange (ISE), the Pacific Exchange (PCX), and the Philadelphia Stock Exchange (PHLX).

Before 1973, options trading was unregulated and options traded over the counter.

Nearly all options are multiply listed, which means they're available for purchase and sale on multiple exchanges. In addition, contract terms and pricing are standardized so that the contracts are **fungible**, or interchangeable. An investor might give an order to purchase an option that is executed on one exchange, and later give an order to sell the same option that is executed on a different exchange.

PHILADELPHIA
STOCK EXCHANGE

CRYING OUT

In the early years of options trading, the floors of exchanges operated as open outcry auctions. Buyers and sellers negotiated directly with each other, using shouts and hand signals to determine prices in a seemingly chaotic—but in reality, very structured—process. Open outcry is similar to the auction system used for stock trading, but relies on a more frenetic negotiating atmosphere.

Today, however, nearly all options transactions take place electronically, and only rare orders above a certain size or those with special contingencies attached are passed on to brokers working on the floor of the exchange. The manner in which a trade is filled is invisible to the investor, regardless of whether it happens electronically or through open outcry. In either case, when a trade has been successfully completed, investors are notified by their brokerage firms.

INTRODUCING MORE PLAYERS

These organizations all have a role to play in options trading:

The Options Clearing Corporation (OCC) is the actual buyer and seller of all listed options contracts, which means that every matched trade is guaranteed by OCC, eliminating any counterparty credit risk.

The Options Industry Council (OIC) is a group sponsored by the options exchanges and OCC. OIC provides education for investors about the benefits and risks of trading options.

The Securities and Exchange Commission (SEC) is a US federal agency that governs the securities industry, including the options industry. The SEC protects investors by enforcing US securities laws and regulating markets and exchanges.

CLEARING THE WAY

One of the innovations that made trading listed options workable from the start was establishing a central clearinghouse to act as issuer and guarantor for all the options contracts in the marketplace.

That clearinghouse, which became The Options Clearing Corporation in 1975, has approximately 140 member firms who clear trades for the brokerage firms, market makers, and customers who buy and sell options.

Because of OCC, investors who open and close positions, trade contracts in the secondary market, or choose to exercise can be confident that their matched trades will be settled on the day following the trade, that premiums will be collected and paid, and that exercise notices will be assigned according to established procedures.

Like the options exchanges, OCC has streamlined the clearing process—evolving from runners who made the rounds of member firms twice each trading day to a totally electronic environment.

What Are the Benefits?

Whether you're hedging, seeking income, or speculating, you can put options to work for your portfolio.

Although options may not be appropriate for everyone, they're among the most flexible of investment choices. Depending on the contract, options can protect or enhance the portfolios of many different kinds of investors in rising, falling, and neutral markets.

REDUCING YOUR RISK

For many investors, options are useful as tools of risk management, acting as insurance policies against a drop in stock prices. For example, if Investor A is concerned that the price of his shares in LMN Corporation is about to drop, he can purchase puts that give him the right to sell his stock at the strike price, no matter how low the market price drops before expiration. At the cost of the option's premium, Investor A has insured himself against losses below the strike price. This type of option practice is also known as **hedging**. While hedging with options may help you manage risk, it's important to remember that all investments carry some risk, and returns are never guaranteed.

Investors who use options to manage risk look for ways to limit potential loss. They may choose to purchase options, since loss is limited to the price paid for the premium. In return, they gain the right to buy or sell the underlying security at an acceptable price for them. They can also profit from a rise in the value of the option's premium, if they choose to sell it back to the market rather than exercise it. Since writers of options are sometimes forced into buying or selling stock at an unfavorable price, the risk associated with certain short positions may be higher.

OPTIONS FOR ALL INVESTORS

Bearish. Investors who anticipate a market downturn can purchase puts on stock to profit from falling prices or to protect portfolios—regardless of whether they hold the stock on which the put is purchased.

Conservative. Investors with a conservative attitude can use options to hedge their portfolios, or act as insurance policies against possible drops in value. Options writing can also be used as a conservative strategy to bolster income. For example, say you would like to own 100 shares of LMN Corporation now trading at $56, and are willing to pay $50 a share. You write an LMN 50 put, and pocket the premium. If prices fall and the option is exercised, you'll buy the shares at $50 each. If prices rise, your option will expire unexercised. If you still decide to buy LMN shares, the higher cost will be offset by the premium you received.

RULE OF THUMB

If you buy a call, you have a **bullish** outlook, and anticipate that the value of the underlying security will rise. If you buy a put you are **bearish**, and think the value of the underlying security will fall.

MODEST PROFITS

Most strategies that options investors use have limited risk but also limited profit potential. For this reason, options strategies are not get-rich-quick schemes. Transactions generally require less capital than equivalent stock transactions, and therefore return smaller dollar figures—but a potentially greater percentage of the investment—than equivalent stock transactions.

A LITTLE DOES A LOT

Options allow holders to benefit from movements in a stock's price at a fraction of the cost of owning that stock. For example: Investors A and B think that stock in company LMN, which is currently trading at $100, will rise in the next few months. Investor A spends $10,000 on the purchase of 100 shares. But Investor B doesn't have much money to invest. Instead of buying

Investor A invests in stock

100 shares of stock, she purchases one LMN call option at a strike price of $115. The premium for the option is $2 a share, or $200 a contract, since each contract covers 100 shares. If the price of LMN shares rises to $120, the value of her option might rise to $5 or higher, and Investor B can sell it for $500, making a $300 profit or a 150% return on her investment. Investor A, who bought 100 LMN shares at $100, could make $2,000, but only realize a 20% return on her investment.

Investor B invests in options

Both invest in LMN at $100 a share

Amount invested = $10,000 Number of shares purchased = 100	Call option with $115 strike Premium = $2 per share 100 shares = 1 contract Contract price = $200 She purchases 1 contract and now has a stake in 100 shares

LMN stock price rises to $120

Her 100 shares are worth $12,000 Profit = $2,000, or 20%	Premium rises to $5 a share New contract price = $500 She sells her option for a profit of $300, or 150%

Long-term. Investors can protect long-term unrealized gains in a stock by purchasing puts that give them the right to sell it at a price that's acceptable to them on or before a particular date. For the cost of the premium, a minimum profit can be locked in. If the stock price rises, the option will expire worthless, but the cost of the premium may be offset by gains to the value of the stock.

Bullish. Investors who anticipate a market upturn can purchase calls on stock to participate in gains in that stock's price—at a fraction of the cost of owning that stock. Long calls can also be used to lock in a purchase price for a particular stock during a bull market, without taking on the risk of price decline that comes with stock ownership.

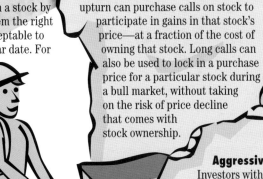

SPECULATIVE CLIMB

Aggressive. Investors with an aggressive outlook use options to leverage a position in the market when they believe they know the future direction of a stock. Options holders and writers can speculate on market movement without committing large amounts of capital. Since options offer leverage to investors, it's possible to achieve a greater percentage return on a given rise or fall than one could through stock ownership. But this strategy can be a risky one, since losses may be larger, and since it is possible to lose the entire amount invested.

Even those investors who use options in **speculative** strategies, such as writing uncovered calls, don't usually realize dramatic returns. The potential profit is limited to the premium received for the contract, and the potential loss is often unlimited. While leverage means the percentage returns can be significant, here, too, the amount of cash changing hands is smaller than with equivalent stock transactions.

What Are the Risks?

The risks of options need to be weighed against their potential returns.

Many options strategies are designed to minimize risk by hedging existing portfolios. While options can act as safety nets, they're not risk free. Since transactions usually open and close in the short term, gains can be realized very quickly. This means that losses can mount quickly as well. It's important to understand all the risks associated with holding, writing, and trading options before you include them in your investment portfolio.

RISKING YOUR PRINCIPAL

Like other securities—including stocks, bonds, and mutual funds—options carry no guarantees, and you must be aware that it's possible to lose all of the principal you invest, and sometimes more. As an options holder, you risk the entire amount of the premium you pay. But as an options writer, you take on a much higher level of risk. For example, if you write an uncovered call, you face unlimited potential loss, since there is no cap on how high a stock price can rise.

However, since initial options investments usually require less capital than equivalent stock positions, your potential cash losses as an options investor are usually smaller than if you'd bought the underlying stock or sold the stock short. The exception to this general rule occurs when you use options to provide leverage: Percentage returns are often high, but it's important to remember that percentage losses can be high as well.

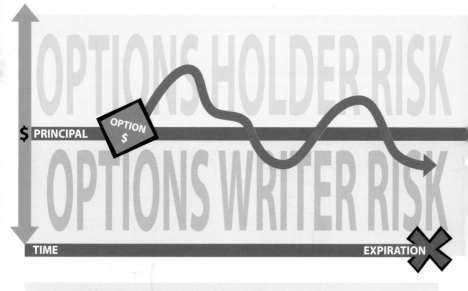

UNDERSTANDING PREMIUM

The value of an equity option is composed of two separate factors. The first, **intrinsic value**, is equal to the amount that the option is in-the-money. Contracts that are at-the-money or out-of-the-money have no intrinsic value. So if you exercised an at-the-money option you wouldn't make money, and you'd lose money if you exercised an out-of-the-money option. Neither would be worth the cost of exercise transaction fees. But all unexercised contracts still have **time value**, which is the perceived—and often changing—dollar value of the time left until expiration. The longer the time until expiration, the higher the time value, since there is a greater chance that the underlying stock price will move and the option will become in-the-money.

Premium = intrinsic value + time value

The entire premium of an at-the-money or out-of-the-money option is its time value, since its intrinsic value is zero. In contrast, the entire premium of an in-the-money option at expiration is its intrinsic value, since the time value is zero.

WASTING TIME

One risk particular to options is **time decay**, because the value of an option diminishes as the expiration date approaches. For this reason, options are considered **wasting assets**, which means that they have no value after a certain date. Stockholders, even if they experience a dramatic loss of value on paper, can hold onto their shares over the long term. As long as the company exists, there is the potential for shares to regain value.

Time is a luxury for stockholders, but a liability for options holders. If the underlying stock or index moves in an unanticipated direction, there is a limited amount of time in which it can correct itself. Once the option expires out-of-the-money it is worthless, and you, as the holder, will have lost the entire premium you paid. Options writers take advantage of this, and usually intend for the contracts they write to expire unexercised and out-of-the-money.

WHAT YOU OWN

It's also important for you as an options investor to understand the difference between owning options and owning stock. Shares of stock are pieces of a company, independent of what their price is now or the price you paid for them. Options are the right to acquire or sell shares of stock at a given price and time. Options holders own the rights to what's sometimes described as price movement, but not a piece of the company.

Shareholders can benefit in ways other than price movement, including the distribution of dividends. They also have the right to vote on issues relating to the management of the company. Options holders don't have those benefits and rights.

THE TAX IMPACT

The tax issues associated with options transactions can be complicated. Any short-term gains you realize on securities you've held for less than a year are taxed at a higher rate than long-term gains, or gains on securities held longer than a year. Since most options are traded or exercised within a matter of weeks, in general the gains you realize will be short term, and may be taxed at the higher rate. But some investors can use short-term losses from options to offset short-term gains on other securities, and reduce their taxes.

Since options contracts can be diverse, the applicable tax rules depend on the particular option, the type of underlying security, and the specifics of the transaction. It's important to consult a professional tax adviser before you begin to trade options, in order to understand how different strategies will affect the taxes you pay.

THE LONG AND SHORT OF IT

In investing, the words **long** and **short** are used to describe what holders and writers, respectively, are doing. When you purchase an option, you are said to have a long position. If you write an option, you have a short position. The same terminology is used to describe ownership of stock: You can **go long** on 100 shares of XYZ by purchasing them, or **go short** by borrowing shares through your brokerage firm and selling them.

PAY ATTENTION

Since options are wasting assets, losses and gains occur in short periods. If you followed a buy and hold strategy, as you might with stocks, you'd risk missing the expiration date or an unexpected event. It's also important to fully understand all potential outcomes of a strategy before you open a position. And once you do, you'll want to be sure to stay on top of changes in your contracts.

- Since an option's premium may change rapidly as expiration nears, you should frequently evaluate the status of your contracts, and determine whether it makes financial sense to close out a position.

- You should be aware of any pending corporate actions, such as splits and mergers, that might prompt contract adjustments. Check OIC's website, www.888options.com, for changes.

How Do You Get Started?

It takes forethought and planning to begin investing successfully in options.

Since there are so many available options—and so many ways to trade them—you might not know where to begin. But getting started is easier than you think, once you determine your goals.

KNOW WHAT YOU WANT...

Before you begin trading options it's critical to have a clear idea of what you hope to accomplish. Options can play a variety of roles in different portfolios, and picking a goal narrows the field of appropriate strategies you might choose. For example, you might decide you want more income from the stocks you own. Or maybe you hope to protect the value of your portfolio from a market downturn. No one objective is better than another, just as no one options strategy is better than another—it depends on your goals.

AND HOW TO GET IT

Once you've decided upon an objective, you can begin to examine options strategies to find one or more that can help you reach that goal. For example, if you want more income from the stocks you own, you might investigate strategies such as writing covered calls. Or, if you're trying to protect your stocks from a market downturn, you might think about purchasing puts, or options on an index that tracks the type of stocks in your portfolio.

MORE THAN JUST A BROKER

Once you're ready to invest in options, you need to choose a brokerage firm. Your firm may offer helpful advice as well as execute your trades. Some firms go further by working with clients to ensure that

1. Open an Account

2. Find Your Level of Options Trading

1	2	3	4	5
Writing covered options	Buying calls, puts, straddles	Debit spreads, cash-secured puts	Credit spreads	Writing naked options, straddles

3. Pick Your Objective

In both visible and invisible ways, **The Options Industry Council (OIC)** and **The Options Clearing Corporation (OCC)** play a part as any investor prepares to trade options for the first time. OIC provides educational material on options trading as well as information about individual options, contract adjustments, and changes in federal regulations. OCC protects investors by guaranteeing every transaction, which means that call holders, for example, don't have to worry that the writer might not fulfill the obligation.

options trading fits into their individual financial plans. They also advise clients about potential objectives and strategies, and outline the risks and benefits of various transactions.

Some options investors choose discount firms that charge lower commissions, but don't offer personalized advising services. But others, including both inexperienced and veteran investors, prefer to consult their brokers before opening or closing out a position.

DOING THE PAPERWORK

Even if you have a general investment account, there are additional steps to take before you can begin trading options. First, you'll have to fill out an options agreement form, which is a document brokerage firms use to measure your knowledge of options and trading strategies, as well as your general investing experience.

Before you begin trading options, you should read the document titled *Characteristics and Risks of Standardized Options*, which contains basic information about options as well as detailed examples of the risks associated with particular contracts and strategies. In fact, your brokerage firm is required to distribute it to all potential options investors.

You can request a free copy of *Characteristics and Risks of Standardized Options* from your firm, order it by calling 888-678-4667, or download a copy at:
- www.888options.com
- www.optionsclearing.com

WATCH THE MARGINS

You can't purchase options **on margin**, as you can with stocks. But some brokerage firms require that certain options transactions, such as writing uncovered calls, take place in a margin account. That means if you write a call, you'll have to keep a balance in your account to cover the cost of purchasing the underlying stocks if the option is exercised. This **margin requirement** for uncovered writers is set at a minimum of 20% of the underlying security minus the amount the option is out-of-the-money, but never less than 10% of the security value.

If the value of the assets in your margin account drops below the required maintenance level, your brokerage firm will make a **margin call**, or notify you that you need to add capital in order to meet the minimum requirements. If you don't take appropriate action, your brokerage firm can liquidate assets in your account without your consent. Since options can change in value over a short period of time, it's important to monitor your account and prevent being caught by a margin call.

4. Choose a Strategy

5. Communicate with Your Brokerage Firm

6. Start Trading

MY OBJECTIVES

WRITE CALLS

PURCHASE PUTS

My Online Broker

WATCH THE MARGIN

ARE YOU ELIGIBLE?

Based on the information you provide in the options agreement, your brokerage firm will approve you for a specific level of options trading. Not all investors are allowed to trade every kind of strategy, since some strategies involve substantial risk. This policy is meant to protect brokerage firms against inexperienced or insufficiently funded investors who might end up defaulting on margin accounts. It may protect investors from trading beyond their abilities or financial means.

The levels of approval and required qualifications vary, but most brokerage firms have four or five levels. In general, the more trading experience under your

RULE OF THUMB
The more time until expiration, the higher the option premium, because the chance of reaching the strike price is greater.

belt, and the more liquid assets you have to invest, the higher your approval level. Firms may also ask you to acknowledge your acceptance of the risks of options trading.

Key Terms and Definitions

Learn the language of the options world.

While many of the terms used to describe buying and selling options are the same terms used to describe other investments, some are unique to options. Mastering the new language may take a little time, but it's essential to understanding options strategies you're considering.

IT'S GREEK TO ME

The terms that estimate changes in the prices of options as various market factors—such as stock price and time to expiration—change are named after Greek letters, and are collectively known as **the Greeks**. Many investors use the Greeks to compare options and find an option that fits a particular strategy. It's important to remember, though, that the Greeks are based on mathematical formulas. While they can be used to assess possible future prices, there's no guarantee that they'll hold true.

GREEKS ON STOCKS

When used to describe stocks, these measurements compare the stock's performance to a benchmark index.

Beta. A measure of how a stock's volatility changes in relation to the over-all market. A beta may help you determine how closely a stock in your portfolio tracks the movement of an index, if you're considering hedging with index options. A beta of 1.5 means a stock gains 1.5 points for every point the index gains—and loses 1.5 points for every point the index loses.

Alpha. A measure of how a stock performs in relation to a benchmark, independent of its beta. A positive alpha means that the stock outperformed what the beta predicted, and a negative alpha means the stock didn't perform as well as predicted.

A VOLATILE SITUATION

Volatility is an important component of an option's price. There are two kinds of volatility: historic and implied. **Historic volatility** is a measure of how much the underlying stock price has moved in the past. The higher the historic volatility, the more the stock price has changed over time. You can use historic volatility as an indication of how much the stock price may fluctuate in the future, but there's no guarantee that past performance will be repeated.

Implied volatility is the percentage of volatility that justifies an option's market price. Investors may use implied volatility to predict how volatile an option will be, but like any prediction, it may or may not hold true.

Volatility is a key element in the time value portion of an option's premium. In general, the higher the volatility—either historic or implied—the higher the option's premium will be. That's because investors assume there's a greater likelihood of the stock price moving before expiration, putting the option in-the-money.

OTHER MEASUREMENTS

Open interest. The number of open positions for a particular options series. High open interest means that there are many open positions on a particular option, but it is not necessarily a sign of bullishness or bearishness.

Volume. The number of contracts—both opening and closing transactions—traded over a certain period. A high daily volume means many investors opened or closed positions on a given day.

Liquidity. The more buyers and sellers in the market, the greater the liquidity for a particular options series. Higher liquidity may mean that there is a demand for a particular option, which might increase the premium if there are lots of buyers, or decrease the premium if there are lots of sellers.

GREEKS ON OPTIONS

When used to describe options, the Greeks usually compare the movement of an option's theoretical price or volatility as the underlying stock changes in price or volatility, or as expiration nears.

Delta. A measure of how much an option price changes when the underlying stock price changes. The delta of an option varies over the life of that option, depending on the underlying stock price and the amount of time left until expiration.

Like most of the Greeks, delta is expressed as a decimal between 0 and +1 or 0 and –1. For example, a call delta of 0.5 means that for every dollar increase in the stock price, the call premium increases 50 cents. A delta between 0 and –1 refers to a put option, since put premiums fall as stock price increases. So a delta of –0.5 would mean that for every dollar increase in the stock price, the put premium would be expected to drop by 50 cents.

Theta. The rate at which premium decays per unit of time as expiration nears. As time decays, options prices can decrease rapidly if they're out-of-the-money. If they're in-the-money near expiration, options price changes tend to mirror those of the underlying stock.

Rho. An estimate of how much the price of an option—its premium—changes when the interest rate changes. For example, higher interest rates may mean that call prices rise and put prices decline.

Vega. An estimate of how much an option price changes when the volatility assumption changes. In general, greater volatility means a higher option premium. Vega is also sometimes referred to as kappa, omega, or tau.

GREEKS ON GREEKS

Some Greeks work as secondary measurements, showing how a particular Greek changes as the option changes in price or volatility.

Gamma. A measure of how much the delta changes when the price of the underlying stock changes. You might think of gamma as the delta of an option's delta.

HEDGING

If you hedge an investment, you protect yourself against losses, usually with another investment that requires additional capital. With options, you might hedge your long stock position by writing a call or purchasing a put on that stock. Hedging is often compared to buying insurance on an investment, since you spend some money protecting yourself against the unexpected.

LEVERAGE

When you leverage an investment, you use a small amount of money to control an investment that's worth much more. Stock investors have leverage when they trade on margin, committing only a percentage of the capital needed and borrowing the rest. As an options investor, you have leverage when you purchase a call, for example, and profit from a change in the underlying stock's price at a lower cost than if you owned the stock. Leverage also means that profits or losses may be higher, when calculated as a percentage of your original investment.

Leverage

Introduction to Options Strategies

Planning, commitment, and research will prepare you for investing in options.

Before you buy or sell options you need a strategy, and before you choose an options strategy, you need to understand how you want options to work in your portfolio. A particular strategy is successful only if it performs in a way that helps you meet your investment goals. If you hope to increase the income you receive from your stocks, for example, you'll choose a different strategy from an investor who wants to lock in a purchase price for a stock she'd like to own.

One of the benefits of options is the flexibility they offer—they can complement portfolios in many different ways. So it's worth taking the time to identify a goal that suits you and your financial plan. Once you've chosen a goal, you'll have narrowed the range of strategies to use. As with any type of investment, only some of the strategies will be appropriate for your objective.

SIMPLE AND NOT-SO-SIMPLE

Some options strategies, such as writing covered calls, are relatively simple to understand and execute. There are more complicated strategies, however, such as spreads and collars, that require two opening transactions. These strategies are often used to further limit the risk associated with options, but they may also limit potential return. When you limit risk, there is usually a trade-off.

Simple options strategies are usually the way to begin investing with options. By mastering simple strategies, you'll prepare yourself for advanced options trading. In general, the more complicated options strategies are appropriate only for experienced investors.

AN OVERVIEW OF STRATEGIES

It's helpful to have an overview of the implications of various options strategies. Once you understand the basics, you'll be ready to learn more about how each strategy can work for you—and what the potential risks are.

	POSSIBLE OBJECTIVE	YOUR MARKET FORECAST
CALL BUYING	Profit from increase in price of the underlying security, or lock in a good purchase price	Neutral to bullish
CALL WRITING	Profit from the premium received, or lower net cost of purchasing a stock	Neutral to bearish, though covered call writing may be bullish
PUT BUYING	Profit from decrease in price of the underlying security, or protect against losses on stock already held	Neutral to bearish
PUT WRITING	Profit from the premium received, or lower net purchase price	Neutral to bullish, though cash-secured puts may be bearish
SPREADS	Profit from the difference in values of the options written and purchased	Bullish or bearish, depending on the particular spread
COLLARS	Protect unrealized profits	Neutral or bullish

MAKE A COMMITMENT

Once you've decided on an appropriate options strategy, it's important to stay focused. That might seem obvious, but the fast pace of the options market and the complicated nature of certain transactions make it difficult for some inexperienced investors to stick to their plan. If it seems that the market or underlying security isn't moving in the direction you predicted, it's possible that you'll minimize your losses by exiting early. But it's also possible that you'll miss out on a future beneficial change in direction.

That's why many experts recommend that you designate an exit strategy or cut-off point ahead of time, and hold firm. For example, if you plan to sell a covered call, you might decide that if the option moves 20% in-the-money before expiration, the loss you'd face if the option were exercised and assigned to you is unacceptable. But if it moves only 10% in-the-money, you'd be confident that there remains enough chance of it moving out-of-the-money to make it worth the potential loss.

A WORD TO THE WISE

By learning some of the most common mistakes that options investors make, you'll have a better chance of avoiding them.

Overleveraging. One of the benefits of options is the potential they offer for leverage. By investing a small amount, you can earn a significant percentage return. It's very important, however, to remember that leverage has a potential downside too: A small decline in value can mean a large percentage loss. Investors who aren't aware of the risks of leverage are in danger of overleveraging, and might face bigger losses than they expected.

Lack of understanding. Another mistake some options traders make is not fully understanding what they've agreed to. An option is a contract, and its terms must be met upon exercise. It's important to understand that if you write a covered call, for example, there is a very real chance that your stock will be called away from you. It's also important to understand how an option is likely to behave as expiration nears, and to understand that once an option expires, it has no value.

Not doing research. A serious mistake that some options investors make is not researching the underlying instrument. Options are derivatives, and their value depends on the price behavior of another financial product—a stock, in the case of equity options. You have to research available options data, and be confident in your reasons for thinking that a particular stock will move in a certain direction before a certain date. You should also be alert to any pending corporate actions such as splits and mergers.

POTENTIAL RISK	POTENTIAL RETURN
Limited to the premium paid	Theoretically unlimited
Unlimited for naked call writing, limited for covered call writing	Limited to the premium received
Limited to the premium paid	Substantial, as the stock price approaches zero
Substantial, as the stock price approaches zero	Limited to the premium received
Limited	Limited
Limited	Limited

Selecting the Right Security

Don't let yourself be overwhelmed by the options.

Choosing a strategy is the first step when investing in options. The second—and equally important—step is finding the right security on which to purchase or write an option. You might choose a stock or another type of equity as the underlying instrument.

The Search for the Right

STOCK ISLANDS

1 INVESTIGATING OPTIONS

When choosing a stock to purchase, you probably look for a company with growth potential or a strong financial outlook—a company whose stock price you think will increase over time or one that will pay regular dividends. But as an options investor, you might be looking for a company whose stock price will rise or one whose price you think will fall in a finite period. What's important is that you correctly predict whether the price will rise or fall, and by how much.

Buying stock also allows you a virtually unlimited amount of time to realize a price gain. As an options holder or writer, however, you need to be accurate in your prediction of the speed with which the stock price will move, as well as how far and in which direction.

2 APPLYING RESEARCH

There's no one best research method for choosing a security when trading options any more than there is when trading stocks. You might prefer a **technical analysis**, which emphasizes an assessment of price trends and trading patterns in market sectors or overall markets, or consult a **fundamental analyst**, who studies the particulars of a certain company.

For example, Investors A and B are both interested in the stock of corporation LMN. They know that a quarterly earnings report will be released in a month, and they'd like to predict whether the stock will rise in response to a good report, or fall in response to low earnings—though, of course, it could do something they don't expect. They both conduct further research. Investor A prefers technical analysis, and looks at statistics such as the market's moving average and the recent performance of LMN's sector, in order to gauge the overall outlook of the company.

Investor B, however, relies on a fundamental analyst who looks at LMN's recent product launches and analyzes the performance of its CEO to predict the nature of the earnings report. Both Investor A and Investor B could

ANALYSIS ALLEY

use their research to estimate whether the earnings report will be good news, neutral, or bad news for LMN, and whether stock will rise or fall in the months after the report's release.

How you apply your research will depend on your style of analysis, as well as your own experience with investing, your knowledge of the stock market, and your intuition. Many experts recommend that you use elements of both technical and fundamental analysis when researching an equity, to get a balanced perspective.

LMN

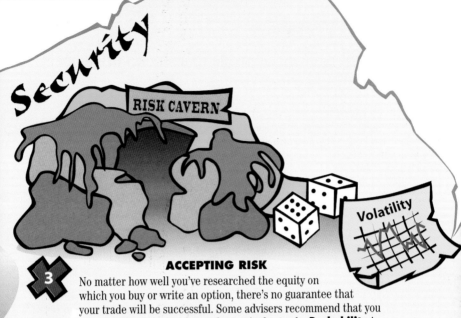

ACCEPTING RISK

3 No matter how well you've researched the equity on which you buy or write an option, there's no guarantee that your trade will be successful. Some advisers recommend that you consider the probability of the success of a particular trade. **Probability** is a measurement of the odds that you'll achieve the goal behind your options strategy, which might be making a profit or purchasing stock, for example.

Probability is based on factors including **volatility**, since an out-of-the-money option on an underlying instrument with high volatility—or one that often changes in price—is more likely to move in-the-money. It's important to estimate the probability of success before committing yourself to a trade. You'll have more realistic expectations and a better sense of what you stand to gain and to lose.

MANAGING YOUR CASH

4 How you're going to manage your capital is another important decision to make before you trade options.

● If you've already allocated all your investment funds to other types of securities, you'll have to reallocate in order to free up capital for options. Most experts recommend that you use options to complement a diversified investment portfolio instead of dedicating your entire trading capital to options.

● If you're not very experienced, you might consider trading options with **risk capital** only, or money that you could tolerate losing entirely, particularly when purchasing simple puts or calls.

● You should also take into account the impact that trading options on margin will have on your cash allocation. If you write an uncovered call, you'll have to deposit a minimum percentage of the value of the underlying shares into a margin account with your broker. This might mean tying up funds that you would have invested elsewhere.

RESEARCH SOURCES

● Financial newspapers, websites, and magazines provide company news and market trends
● Your broker or financial adviser can make recommendations as well as provide professional research
● Options newsletters often offer information on particular equities and trading strategies

Call Buying

You can profit from an increase in a stock's price by purchasing a call.

Buying calls is popular with options investors, novices and experts alike. The strategy is simple: You buy calls on a stock or other equity whose market price you think will be higher than the strike price plus the premium by the expiration date. Or, you buy a call whose premium you think will increase enough to outpace time decay. In either case, if your expectation is correct, you may be in a position to realize a positive return. If you're wrong, you face the loss of your premium—generally much less than if you had purchased shares and they lost value.

INVESTOR OBJECTIVES

Call buying may be appropriate for meeting a number of different objectives. For example, if you'd like to establish a price at which you'll buy shares at some point in the future, you may buy call options on the stock without having to commit the full investment capital now.

Or, you might use a buy low/sell high strategy, buying a call that you expect to rise and hoping to sell it after it increases in value. In that case, it's key to pick a call that will react as you expect, since not all calls move significantly even when the underlying stock rises.

CALLING FOR LEVERAGE

One major appeal of purchasing calls is the possibility of leveraging your investment, and realizing a much higher percentage return than if you made the equivalent stock transaction.

1 Investor A buys 100 shares of company LMN stock at $10 each, investing a total of $1,000.

```
    100 Shares
x $   10 Per share
= $1,000 Investment
```

2 In the next year, the stock rises in value to $15.

1 Investor B, however, invests the same $1,000 in options, buying 20 calls at a strike price of $12.50. Each call cost her $50, or 50 cents per share, since her contract covers 100 shares.

CALLS
$50 (50¢ per share)

Strike price
$12.50

```
$     50 Per call
x     20 Calls
= $1,000 Investment
```

2 When the stock goes up to $15, her options are in-the-money by $2.50.
Therefore the value of her calls rises from 50 cents at purchase to at least $2.50 per share, a $200 gain per contract.

PERFECT TIMING

Buying calls can provide an advantage over several different time periods:

Short term. Investors can profit if they sell an option for more than they paid for it, for example if there is an increase in the stock's price before expiration.

Medium term. Over a matter of several months, investors can use call options to minimize the risk of owning stock in an uncertain market. Investors who want to lock in a purchase price for a year or longer can buy LEAPS, or periodically purchase new options.

Long term. LEAPS allow investors to purchase calls at a strike price they're comfortable with, and accumulate the capital to purchase those shares in the intervening time until expiration.

Some experienced investors may purchase calls in order to hedge against short sales of stock they've made. Investors who sell short hope to profit from a decrease in the stock's price. If the shares increase in value instead, they can face heavy losses. Buying calls allows short sellers to protect themselves against the unexpected increase, and limit their potential risk.

EXERCISING YOUR CALLS

Most call contracts are sold before expiration, allowing their holders to realize a profit if there are gains in the premium. If you've purchased a call with the intent of owning the underlying instrument, however, you can exercise your right at any time before expiration, subject to the exercise cut-off policies of your brokerage firm.

However, if you don't resell and don't exercise before expiration, you'll face the loss of all of the premium you paid. If your call is out-of-the-money at expiration, you most likely won't exercise. If your option is at-the-money, transaction fees may make it not worth exercising. But if your option is in-the-money, you should be careful not to let expiration pass without acting.

CHOOSING A SECURITY

In general, purchasing calls indicates a bullish sentiment, so you should consider a stock or stock index whose price you think is set to rise. This might be a stock you feel will rise in the short term, allowing you to profit from an increase in premium. You might also look for a stock with long-term growth potential that you'd like to own. Purchasing calls allows you to lock in an acceptable price, at the cost of the premium you pay.

3 Investor A sells and makes $500, or a 50% return on his initial investment.

```
   100 Shares
x $    15 Per share
= $1,500 Sale price
```

$1,500 Sale price
−$1,000 Investment
= $ 500 Profit or
           50% return

However, if the stock price falls at expiration to $9, Investor A will lose $100, or 10% of his investment. Investor B will lose $1,000, or 100% of her investment.

3 At expiration the 20 contracts are now worth $5,000, or $4,000 above what she invested, a 400% return.

CALLS
$250 ($2.50 per share)

```
$   250 Per call
x      20 Calls held
= $5,000 Sale price
```

$5,000 Sale price
−$1,000 Investment
= $4,000 Profit or
          400% return

BETTER THAN MARGIN

For certain investors, buying calls is an attractive alternative to buying stock on margin. Calls offer the same leverage that you can get from buying on margin, but you take on less potential risk.

If you buy stock on margin, you must maintain a certain reserve of cash in your margin account to cover the possible loss in value of those stocks. If the stock price does fall, you must add cash to meet the margin requirement, liquidate a portion of your position, or face having your brokerage firm liquidate your assets.

If you purchase calls, you have the same benefit of low initial investment as the margin trader, but if the value of the stock drops, the main risk you face is loss of the premium, an amount that's usually much smaller than the initial margin requirement.

Call Writing

You can write covered calls to earn income on your stocks.

Writing calls is a straightforward options strategy. When you write a call, you receive cash up front and, in most cases, hope that the option is never exercised. It can be conservative or risky, depending on whether you're covered or uncovered.

INVESTOR OBJECTIVES

You might write calls in order to receive short-term income from the premium you'll be paid. If that's your strategy, you anticipate that the option you write will expire out-of-the-money, and won't be exercised. In that case, you'll retain all of the premium as profit. If you've written this call on stocks you already own, known as a **covered call**, the premium can act as a virtual dividend that you receive on your assets. Many investors use this strategy as a way to earn additional income on nondividend-paying stocks.

Alternately, you could view the premium as a way to reduce your cost basis, or the amount that you paid for each share of stock.

CALCULATING RETURN

In order to calculate the return on a written call, you'll have to take into account the transaction costs and brokerage fees you pay for opening the position, which will be deducted from the premium you receive. And if your option is exercised, you'll have to pay another round of fees. But since you probably plan for your option to expire unexercised, if you're successful you won't face any exit transaction fees or commission.

If you write a call on stock you hold in a margin account, you should consider the margin requirement imposed by your firm when calculating return. If your trade is successful you retain all of your capital, but it will be tied up in the margin account until expiration. That means you can't invest it elsewhere in the meantime.

COVERED CALLS

1 When you write a covered call, you own the stock. For example, say you purchased 100 shares of LMN stock at $50.

```
    100 Shares
x $   50 Per share
= $5,000 Investment
```

CALL
$55
($3 per share)

$300

2 You write a 55 call on the stock, and receive a $300 premium, or $3 for each share covered by this contract.

NAKED CALLS

A much more risky strategy is writing **naked calls**, or options on stock you don't own. Also known as **uncovered call writing**, this strategy appeals to bearish investors who want to capitalize on a decline in the underlying shares.

$300

1 You write a 55 call on a stock, and receive a $300 premium, or $3 for each share covered by this contract.

CALL
$55
($3 per share)

2 If the price doesn't go up and the option expires unexercised, you keep the $300 premium as profit.

If you have written an option on a stock with an upcoming dividend distribution, it's important to know that the likelihood of exercise is much higher right before a dividend payout. If the stock's dividend date on a call you've written is approaching, you should re-evaluate and determine whether to close out your position.

EXITING AND EXERCISE

If the stock or other equity on which you wrote a call begins to move in the opposite direction from what you anticipated, you can close out your position by buying a call in the same series as the one you sold. The premium you pay may be more or less than the premium you received, depending on the call's intrinsic value and the time left until expiration, among other factors. You can also close out your position and then write new calls with a later expiration, a strategy known as **rolling out**.

If the call you wrote is exercised—as is possible at any point before expiration—you will have to deliver the underlying security to your brokerage firm. The **assignment** for an exercised call is made by OCC to any of its member brokerage firms. If your brokerage firm receives an assignment on an options series on which you hold a short position, you may be selected to fulfill the terms of the contract if you were the first at your brokerage firm to open the position, or by random selection, depending on the policy of the firm. It is extremely rare for the writer of an in-the-money call to not have to sell the underlying stock at expiration.

COVERED CALLS

Writing covered calls is a popular options strategy. If you buy shares at the same time that you write calls on them, the transaction is known as a **buy-write**. If you write calls on shares you already hold, it is sometimes called an **overwrite**. This strategy combines the benefits of stock ownership and options trading, and each aspect provides some risk protection for the other. If you write a covered call, you retain your shareholder rights, which means you'll receive dividends and be able to vote on the company's direction.

Writing covered calls is a way to receive additional income from stocks you already own. It can also offer limited downside protection against unrealized gains on stocks you've held for some time, since you lock in a price at which to sell the stock, should the option be exercised.

You should realize, however, that if a stock on which you've written a covered call rises in value, there's a very real chance that your option will be exercised, and you'll have to turn over your shares, missing out on potential gains above the strike price of your option.

③ That means that the $50 you paid for each share is offset by the $3 you received, so your **net price paid** is actually $47 per share.

$5,000
− $ 300
= $4,700
or $ 47 **Per share**

④ Even if the option is exercised, you'll receive $55 per share, which is a profit of $8 per share, or $800.

$5,500
− $4,700
= $ 800 **Profit**

However, if the stock price rises significantly above $55, you won't share in that gain.

③ If the stock price goes up to $59 and the 55 call is exercised, you receive $55 a share or $5,500. But you'll have to buy the stock at market price, or $5,900. The premium reduces your $400 loss to $100.

$5,900 **Purchase**
− $5,500 **Exercise**
= $ 400
− $ 300 **Premium**
= $ 100 **Net loss**

While this loss is moderate, every additional dollar that the stock price increases means your loss increases by $100—and there's no limit to how high your loss could climb.

If you choose this strategy, you'll have to keep the minimum cash margin requirement in your margin account, to cover the possibly steep losses you face if the option is exercised. If you are assigned, you must purchase the underlying stock in order to deliver it and fulfill your obligation under the contract.

Put Buying

You can hedge your stock positions by going long with puts.

Buying puts is a simple strategy that can help protect your assets or let you profit even in a bear market. If you think the market is going to decline, buying puts might be more advantageous than either selling the stocks you own or selling stock short through your margin account.

INVESTOR OBJECTIVES

Put buying is a strategy some investors use to hedge existing stock positions. For the cost of the premium, you can lock in a selling price, protecting yourself against any drop in asset value below the strike price until the option expires. If you exercise your option, the put writer must purchase your shares at the strike price, regardless of the stock's current market price.

But if the stock price rises, you're still able to benefit from the increase since you can let the option expire and hold onto your shares. Your maximum loss, in that case, is limited to the amount you paid for the premium.

Speculators who forecast a bearish equity market often buy puts in order to profit from a market downturn. As the price of the underlying equity decreases, the value of the put option theoretically rises, and it can be sold at a profit. The potential loss is predetermined—and usually smaller—which makes buying puts more appealing than another bearish trading strategy, selling stock short.

GETTING MARRIED

If you buy shares of the underlying stock at the same time that you purchase a put, the strategy is known as a **married put**. If you purchase a put on an equity that you've held for some time, the strategy is known as a **protective put**. Both of these strategies combine the benefits of stock ownership—dividends and a shareholder's vote—with the downside protection that a put provides.

Holding the underlying stock generally indicates a bullish market opinion, in contrast to other long put positions. If you would like to continue owning a stock, and think it will rise in value, a married put can act as an insurance policy in case the stock price drops, minimizing the risks associated with stock ownership. In the same way, a protective put locks in unrealized gains on stocks you've held, in case they begin to lose value.

SHORT A STOCK OR LONG A PUT

If you **sell stock short**, you borrow shares on margin from your brokerage firm and sell them on the stock market. If—as you hope—the stock price drops, you buy the equivalent number of shares back at a lower price, and repay your brokerage firm. The difference in the two prices is your profit from the trade. For many investors, buying puts is an attractive alternative to shorting stock.

Shorting stock requires a margin account with your brokerage firm. A short seller also faces the possibility of a margin call if the stock price rises, and could be forced to sell off other assets.	Puts are purchased outright, usually for a much lower amount than the margin requirement, so you don't have to commit as much cash to the trade.
Shorting stock involves potentially unlimited loss if the price of the stock begins to rise and the shares have to be repurchased at a higher price than they were sold.	A long put poses much less risk to an investor than shorting stock. The holder of a put always faces a predetermined, limited amount of risk.
Investors can only short stock on an uptick, or upward price movement. The uptick rule is meant to prevent a rush of selling as the price of a security drops.	Puts can be purchased regardless of a stock's current market price.

CALCULATING

Whenever you buy a put, your maximum loss is limited to the amount you paid for the premium. That means calculating the potential loss for a long put position is as simple as adding any fees or commissions to the premium you paid. You'll realize this loss if the option expires unexercised or out-of-the-money.

RETURN

If you anticipate experiencing a loss and sell your option before expiration, you may be able to make back some of the premium you paid and reduce your loss, though the market price of the option will be less than the premium you paid.

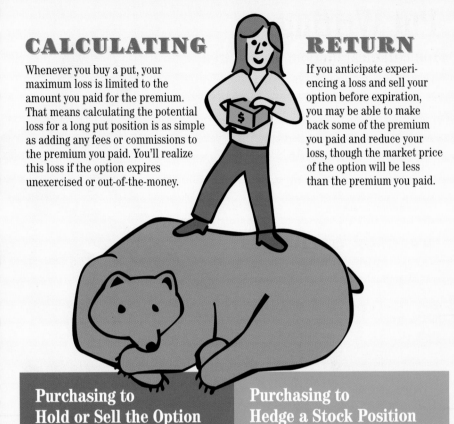

Purchasing to Hold or Sell the Option

If you purchase a put and later sell it, you can calculate return by figuring the difference between what you paid and what you received.

For example, say you purchase one LMN put for $300, or $3 per share.

A month later, the price of the underlying equity falls, placing the put in-the-money. You sell your option for $600, or $6 per share.

Your return is $300, or 100% of your investment.

$600	**Sale price**
– $300	**LMN put price**
= $300	**or 100% return**

If the price of the stock has risen after a month, the put is out-of-the-money, and the premium drops to $200.

You decide to cut your losses and sell the put. You've lost $100, or 33% of your investment.

$300	**LMN put price**
– $200	**Sale price**
= $100	**or 33% loss**

Purchasing to Hedge a Stock Position

If you purchased the put to hedge a stock position, calculating your return means finding the difference between your total investment—the price of the premium added to the amount you paid for the shares—and what you would receive if you exercised your option.

For example, if you purchased 100 LMN shares at $40 each, you invested $4,000.

If you purchased one LMN put with a strike price of $35 for $200, or $2 per share, you've invested $4,200 total in the transaction.

If you exercise the option, you'll receive $3,500, for a $700 loss on your $4,200 investment.

$4,200	**Total investment**
– $3,500	**Receive at exercise**
= $ 700	**Loss**

A $700 loss might seem big, but keep in mind that if the price of the stock falls below $35, you would face a potentially significant loss if you didn't hold the put. By adding $200 to your investment, you've guaranteed a selling price of $35, no matter how low the market price drops.

Put Writing

You can earn income or lock in a purchase price with a put.

While writing puts can sometimes be a risky transaction, there is room for the strategy in even conservative portfolios. By writing puts on stocks you'd like to own, you can lock in a purchase price for a set number of shares. But if the stock price increases, you may still profit from the premium you receive.

INVESTOR OBJECTIVES

Investors who choose to write puts are often seeking additional income. If you have a neutral to bullish prediction for a certain stock or stock index, you can sell a put on that underlying instrument, and you'll be paid a premium. If the underlying instrument doesn't drop in price below the strike price, the option will most likely expire unexercised. The premium is your profit on the transaction.

For example, say you think that the stock of LMN, currently trading at $52, won't drop below $50 in the next few months.

You could write one LMN put with a strike price of $45, set to expire in six months, and sell it for $200. If the price of LMN rises, stays the same, or even drops to $46,

CALCULATING RETURN

If you write a put and it expires unexercised, your return may seem simple to calculate: Subtract any fees and commissions from the premium you received. But writing puts usually requires a margin account with your brokerage firm, so you should include in your calculations any investing capital that was held in that account, since it could perhaps have been profitably invested elsewhere during the life of the option.

For example, if you write the LMN 45 put, you'd receive $200. But your brokerage firm would require that premium, along with a percentage of the $4,500 needed to purchase the shares, to be held

on reserve in your margin account. The capital is still yours, but it is tied up until the put expires or you close out your position.

If you write a put that is exercised, the premium you receive when you open the position reduces the amount that you pay for the shares when you meet your obligation to buy. In the case of the

Write Put for Income

$51
$50
$49
$48 $200 PUT   OUT-OF-THE-MONEY
$47
$46
Strike Price $45 Keep the $200
$44
$43
$42
$41
TIME   EXPIRATION

RISKY BUSINESS

Writing options is generally considered riskier than holding options.

- With any put writing transaction, your maximum profit is limited to the amount of premium you receive.

- If you decide to close out your position before expiration, you might have to buy back your option at a higher price than what you received for selling it.

- At exercise, the potential loss you face is substantial if the price of the underlying instrument falls below the strike price of the put.

Due to the risks involved, and the complications of margin requirements, writing puts is an options strategy that may be most appropriate for experienced investors.

your option remains out-of-the-money. You'll keep the $200.

A more conservative use of put writing combines the options strategy with stock ownership. If you have a target price for a particular stock you'd like to own, you could write put options at an acceptable strike price. You'd receive the premium at the opening of the transaction, and if the option is exercised before expiration, you'll have to buy the shares. The premium you received, however, will reduce your **net price paid** on those shares.

For example, if the price of LMN stock drops to $42, your short put with a strike of $45 is in-the-money. If you are assigned, you'll have to purchase the stock for $4,500. That amount is partially offset by the $200 premium, so your total outlay is $4,300.

You would pay a net price of $43 for each share of LMN stock. If its price rises in the future, you could realize significant gains.

Or, you could close out your position prior to assignment by purchasing the same put. Since the option is now in-the-money, however, its premium may rise to $300, making your loss $100.

Write Put to Own Stock

Buy back the put for $300 with a loss of $100, or purchase the stock.

$200 PUT

IN-THE-MONEY

EXPIRATION

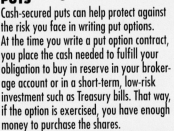

CASH-SECURED PUTS

Cash-secured puts can help protect against the risk you face in writing put options. At the time you write a put option contract, you place the cash needed to fulfill your obligation to buy in reserve in your brokerage account or in a short-term, low-risk investment such as Treasury bills. That way, if the option is exercised, you have enough money to purchase the shares.

Securing your put with cash also prevents you from writing more contracts than you can afford, since you'll commit all the capital you'll need up front.

LMN 45 put, the $200 premium reduces what you pay for the stock from $4,500 to $4,300. If you plan to hold the shares you purchase in your portfolio, then your cost basis is $43 per share plus commissions.

If you don't want to hold those shares, you can sell them in the stock market. But if you sell them for less than $43 per share, you'll have a loss.

Spread Strategies

You can limit your exposure using two or more options on the same stock.

A spread is an options strategy that requires two transactions, usually executed at the same time. You purchase one option and write another option on the same stock or index. Both options are identical except for one element, such as strike price or expiration date. The most common are **vertical spreads**, in which one option has a higher strike price than the other. The difference between the higher strike price and the lower strike price is also known as the **spread**. Different spread strategies are appropriate for different market forecasts.

You use a **bear spread** if you anticipate a decline in the stock price. You use a **bull spread** if you anticipate an increase in the stock price.

HOW YOU HEDGE WITH SPREADS

If stock LMN is trading at $45:

Investor A sells a call with a strike price of $40, and purchases a call with a strike price of $55. She receives $720 for the call she sells, since it is in-the-money, and pays only $130 for the call she purchases, since it is out-of-the-money. Her cash received, or net credit, so far is $590.

Investor B writes a 40 call on LMN, and receives $720. His net investment is the margin his brokerage firm requires for a naked call.

INVESTOR A

Write 40 call

Purchase 55 call

INVESTOR B

Each options transaction is known as a **leg** of the overall strategy, and most options spreads stand on two legs—though there are some strategies with three or more legs.

WHAT ARE THE BENEFITS?

Many options investors use spreads because they offer a double hedge, which means that both profit and loss are limited. Investors who are interested in more aggressive options strategies that might expose them to significant potential losses can hedge those risks by making them one leg of a spread. The trade-off is that the potential profit is limited as well.

It might help to think of spreads in terms of insurance. Just as you can open an options position to protect against losses in a stock position, you can open an options position to protect against losses in another options position.

CREDIT OR DEBIT?

If, like Investor A, you receive more money for the option you write than you pay for the option you buy, you've opened a **credit spread**. The difference between the two premiums is a credit you receive, and it will be deposited in your brokerage account when you open the position. In most cases, the goal of a credit spread is to have both options expire worthless, retaining your credit as profit from the transaction.

If you pay more for your long option than you receive for your short option, you're taking on a **debit spread**. You'll have to pay your brokerage firm the difference between the two premiums when you open the transaction.

In most cases, the goal of a debit spread is to have the stock move beyond the strike price of the short option so that you realize the maximum value of the spread.

MORE TYPES OF SPREADS

A **calendar** spread is the purchase of one option and writing of another with a different expiration date, rather than with a different strike price. This is usually a neutral strategy.

A **straddle** is the purchase or writing of both a call and a put on an underlying instrument with the same strike price and the same expiration date. A buyer expects the underlying stock to move significantly, but isn't sure about the direction. A seller, on the other hand, hopes that the underlying price remains stable at the strike price.

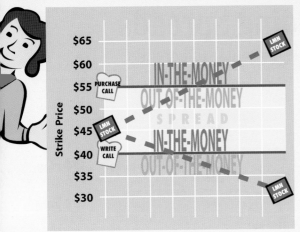

If the stock price rises to $60 at expiration:
Investor A's short call is in-the-money, and she must sell 100 LMN shares at $40 each. However, her long call is in-the-money as well, which means she can buy those same shares for $55 each. Her net loss for each share is $15, or $1,500 total. This is offset by the premium she received, reducing her maximum potential loss to $910.

If the stock price falls below $40 at expiration:
Both of Investor A's options expire out-of-the-money, and she keeps the $590 for the maximum profit.

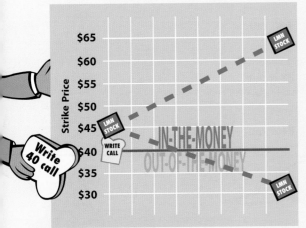

If the stock price rises to $60 at expiration:
Investor B's short call is in-the-money, and he must sell 100 LMN shares at $40 each, for a total loss of $2,000 over their market price. His credit offsets this by $720, reducing his maximum potential loss to $1,280.

If the stock price falls below $40 at expiration:
Investor B's option expires out-of-the-money, and he keeps his entire $720.

Credit spread:
premium you receive > premium you pay

Debit spread:
premium you receive < premium you pay

ARE YOU QUALIFIED?

Although spreads aren't always speculative or aggressive, they are complex strategies that aren't appropriate for all investors. Your brokerage firm may have its own approval levels for debit spreads and credit spreads, to ensure that you're financially qualified and have adequate investing experience. Additionally, managing spreads as expiration nears requires time and attention, so you should be sure you want to take on the challenge.

A **strangle** is the purchase or writing of a call and a put with the same expiration date and different—but both out-of-the-money—strike prices. A strangle holder hopes for a large move in either direction, and a strangle writer hopes for no significant move in either direction.

EXECUTING A STRATEGY

1 The first step in executing a spread is choosing an underlying security on which to purchase and write the options.

2 Next, you'll have to choose the strike prices and expiration dates that you think will be profitable. That means calculating how far you think a stock will move in a particular direction, as well as how long it will take to do so.

3 You should be sure to calculate the maximum profit and maximum loss for your strategy, as well as the circumstances under which you might experience them. Having realistic expectations is essential to smart options investing.

4 Finally, you'll have to make the transactions through a margin account with your brokerage firm. The minimum margin requirement for a spread is usually the difference between the two strike prices times the number of shares covered.

Understanding Spreads

Bulls and bears, calls and puts, and credits and debits don't have to be confusing.

There are four common vertical spread strategies: the bull put, the bull call, the bear put, and the bear call. Each of these has one long leg, or an option you buy, and one short leg, or an option you write.

Many brokerage firms permit you to enter both legs of a transaction simultaneously. With others, you must execute separate transactions in an approved sequence.

	Credit or debit?	Long leg	Short leg
Bull put	Credit	Put at lower strike	Put at higher strike
Bull call	Debit	Call at lower strike	Call at higher strike
Bear put	Debit	Put at higher strike	Put at lower strike
Bear call	Credit	Call at higher strike	Call at lower strike

EXIT A SPREAD

When you exit a spread, both legs are usually closed out, rather than exercised, since buying and selling the underlying stock means committing large amounts of capital to the strategy. Instead, you might close out the spread, by making an offsetting purchase of the option you wrote, and an offsetting sale of the option you had originally purchased.

For example, if you were moderately bullish on stock LMN, which is trading at $55, you might open a **bull call spread**. You could buy a 60 call for $350 and write a 65 call, receiving $150. Your net debit is $200, which is also your maximum loss if the stock price stays below $60.

If the options stay out-of-the-money

$350	Purchase of 60 call
– $150	Receive on 65 call
= $200	Net debit

If the price of the stock rises to $66 at expiration, both options will be in-the-money, and it's reasonable to assume the option you wrote will be exercised. If that's the case, you can exercise your long call and purchase 100 LMN shares for $6,000, and then sell those shares for $6,500 to meet your short 65 call assignment. If

exercise and assignment occurred at expiration, your firm would probably net the difference.

You'd earn $500, and after subtracting the

If the options are in-the-money

$6,500	Sell shares
– $6,000	Purchase shares
= $ 500	Proceeds
– $ 200	Debit
= $ 300	Profit

debit of $200, your profit would be $300. You would have invested $200 for that $300 profit. Alternatively, at or near expiration, you could close out your short call by buying it back for about $100 and selling your long call for about $600, leaving you with a profit of about $300, after the initial $200 debit.

You committed only $300 in cash (the debit plus the cost of offsetting your short call), instead of the $6,000 necessary if you were to exercise your long call. Either way, you have given up the opportunity to profit if the stock continues to rise.

Market forecast	Max profit	Max loss
Neutral or bullish	Net credit	Spread times 100, less credit
Moderately bullish	Spread times 100, less debit	Net debit
Moderately bearish	Spread times 100, less debit	Net debit
Neutral or bearish	Net credit	Spread times 100, less credit

OFFSET YOUR LOSSES

Offsetting your spread position, or buying back the spread you sold, can be advantageous if the underlying stock has moved against you. If you are bearish on LMN when it is trading at $55, you might open a **bear call spread**.

You can purchase a 65 call for $150, and sell a 60 call, receiving $350. Your net credit is $200, which is also the amount of your maximum profit, if LMN stays below $60 and both options expire out-of-the-money.

If the options expire out-of-the-money

$350	Receive on 60 call
− $150	Purchase of 65 call
= $200	Net credit

If your expectations were wrong and the stock price rises to $66, both LMN options will be in-the-money. At or near expiration, you might sell your 65 call for

EARNING INCOME

Spreads can also be used to create income from stocks you hold.

For example, say you bought 100 LMN shares at $50. Now the stock is trading at $30, and you don't think it will rise much in the near future.

You'd like to receive income on your shares, but you don't want to have them called away from you, incurring a loss for the tax year.

You write a slightly out-of-the-money call at $32.50, receiving $250. You simultaneously buy a 35 call for $150. Your net credit is $100.

If the options stay out-of-the-money

$250	Receive on 32.50 call
− $150	Purchase of 35 call
= $100	Net credit

If the price of the stock stays below $32.50, you pocket the $100.

If the stock price increases above $35, you can close out both options positions at a loss of $250 (the amount of the spread times the number of shares covered), which is reduced to $150 after accounting for your credit. This loss is one you may be willing to accept as your shares of LMN gain value.

If the options are in-the-money

100	Number of shares
x $ 2.50	Amount of the spread
= $ 250	Loss
− $ 100	Credit
= $ 150	Net loss

$100, and buy back the 60 call for $600. The loss of $500 would be partially offset by the original $200 credit.

If the stock is $66 at expiration, you can assume your short call will be assigned, obligating you to sell 100 LMN shares at $6,000. You'd exercise your long call, and buy 100 LMN shares for $6,500. Your firm would probably net the difference, creating a $500 loss in your account that would be partially offset by your original $200 credit.

If the options are in-the-money

$600	Buy back 60 call
− $100	Sell 65 call
= $500	Loss
− $200	Credit
= $300	Net loss

Collar Transactions

You can use a collar to rein in profits you haven't yet realized, but you might have to give up future gains in return.

A **collar** is a spread strategy designed to protect unrealized profits on stock you already own. You purchase a protective put on your long stock position, and offset the cost of that put by writing a call that is covered by your long stock position. The collar spread is also known as a **fence** for the protection it provides.

In most cases, both the long put and the short call are out-of-the-money. If the call you write is less expensive than the put you buy, you'll pay more premium than you receive, and will establish a **debit collar**. If the put you buy is less expensive than the call you write, you'll receive more premium than you pay, and will establish a **credit collar**.

RULE OF THUMB

Call and put options move in opposition. Call options usually rise in value as the underlying market prices go up. Put options usually rise in value as the market prices go down—but time decay and a change in volatility also have an effect.

INVESTOR OBJECTIVES

A collar is most often used as a protective strategy. If you hold a stock that has made significant gains, you might want to lock in those gains, protecting your position against a future drop in price. Writing a covered call can fully or partially offset the cost of purchasing a protective put. Just as with other spread strategies, the risk you face with a collar is limited—and, in return, so is the potential profit.

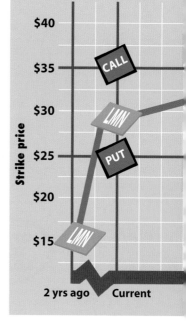

For example, say you purchased 100 shares of LMN at $15 two years ago, and its current market price is $30.

```
    100  Shares
x $  15  Per share
= $1,500 Original cost
```

LOSS

If you purchase a 25 put, you'll have the right to sell those shares at $25 before expiration, locking in a $10 profit on each share, or a total of $1,000. Suppose that put costs you $275, or $2.75 per share.

Let's say you also write a 35 call with the same expiration month, and receive $250 in premium, or $2.50 per share.

```
  $275  Put price paid
- $250  Call price received
= $ 25  Net cost
```

If the price of LMN rises above $35 at expiration, your call most likely will be exercised. You'll receive $3,500 for your shares, or a $2,000 profit, but you'll miss out on any further gains the stock may have.

Since the put you purchased cost more than the call you wrote, your net cost is $25—less than one tenth of the price of the protective put alone. It would cost you only $25 to ensure that you could sell at a

PROFIT

IN-THE-MONEY

OUT-OF-THE-MONEY

OUT-OF-THE-MONEY

IN-THE-MONEY

LMN

EXPIRATION

YOUR OPTIONS AT EXPIRATION

Depending on the direction the stock moves, your choices at expiration of the legs of your collar vary:

If the price of the stock rises above the strike price of the short call:
If assigned, you can fulfill your short call obligation and sell your shares at the strike price. You'll lock in profits over what you initially paid for the stock, but you'll miss out on any gains above the strike price. Alternately, you could close out your position by purchasing the same call you sold, quite possibly at a higher price than what you paid for it. This may be worth it if the difference in premiums is less than the additional profit you anticipate you'll realize from gains in the stock's value, or if one of your goals is to retain the stock.

If the price of the stock remains between both strikes:
You can let your put expire unexercised, or sell it back, most likely for less than what you paid, since its premium will have decreased from time decay. Your short call will probably expire unexercised, which means you keep the entire premium. Depending on whether your collar was a credit or debit spread, you'll retain your initial credit as a profit, or debit as a loss.

If the price of the stock falls below the strike price of the long put:
By exercising your put, you can sell your shares at the strike price. Your short call will probably expire unexercised, and you keep all of the proceeds from the sale of the call.

When executing a collar, it's important to define your range of return, or the strike prices for both the put you purchase and the call you write. The strike price of the protective put should be high enough to lock in most of your unrealized profit. The strike price of the covered call should be high enough to allow you to participate in some upward price movement, but not so far out-of-the-money that the premium you receive does little to offset the cost of your protective put.

minimum profit of $10 per share, or $1,000 per contract.

In most cases, a collar works best if you have a neutral to bearish market forecast for a stock that has behaved bullishly in the past, leaving you with unrealized gains you'd like to protect. Some investors use collars as income-producing strategies by selling them for a credit. While that approach can be profitable, it also requires time and attention to manage the strategy.

COMMISSIONS AND FEES
As with stock transactions, options trades incur commissions and fees charged by your brokerage firm to cover the cost of executing a trade. You'll pay fees when opening a position as well as when exiting. The amount of these charges varies from brokerage firm to brokerage firm, so you should check with yours before executing any transaction. Be sure to account for fees when calculating the potential profit and loss you face.

You should also keep in mind that spread transactions that require two legs mean you may face double commissions at entry. And it also helps to consider that any strategy that ends with an unexercised option, such as a covered call, means—if you're not assigned—you won't pay any commissions or fees at exit.

Exit Strategies

The best time to plan your exit is before you've entered.

You can exit an options strategy at any point before expiration, and you may have more than one alternative. But the exit strategy you choose and your timing in putting it into effect might mean the difference between a profit and a loss, a small profit and a bigger one, or a small loss and a bigger one. Smart investing means establishing how you'll exit if your option is in-the-money, at-the-money, or out-of-the-money—before you open the trade.

consequences of selling or acquiring stock through the exercise of an option, since it might affect your capital gains or losses for the year.

If you're an options holder, you'll have more flexibility when deciding how to exit, since you have the choice not to exercise. You might still close out your position by selling the option, rather than exercising it. If the option's premium has gone up since you bought it, closing out would

CLOSING UP SHOP

Since you can close out your position, or buy back an option you sold, as an options writer you're almost never forced to fulfill an obligation to buy or sell the underlying instrument—assuming you close out before expiration. Keep in mind, though, that in-the-money stock options are often exercised before expiration. If you write an option, closing out is the only way to make sure you won't be assigned. Depending on the option's premium when you want to buy it back, you might pay less than you received, making a net profit. But you might also have to pay more than you received, taking a net loss.

If that loss is less than what you would have faced were the option exercised, closing out might be the best exit. You should also keep in mind the tax

CHOICES FOR OPTIONS HOLDERS

CALL

If you're long an option, the price you paid in premium might reduce your gains. For example, if you hold an LMN 90 call that cost you $200, you'll have to factor in the $2 per share you spent on the option when deciding how and when to exit:

CHOICES FOR OPTIONS WRITERS

PUT

If you're short an option, the premium you received will add to your gain or reduce your loss. For example, if you wrote an LMN 90 put that earned you $200, you can factor in the $2 per share you received for the option:

IN-THE-MONEY

If the stock price is above $92

- Your option is in-the-money. You can exercise and buy shares for $90. You can then retain the stock or possibly sell it on the market for more than $92, offsetting the $200 you spent, and still making a profit.
- You can possibly sell the option for more than the $200 you paid for it, making a profit. Investors who purchase options for leverage often choose this exit strategy.

If the stock price is below $88

- The option is in-the-money, and will most likely be exercised, which means you'll have to buy 100 shares for more than their market price, taking a loss.
- You might buy the option back before it is exercised, paying more for it than you received, and taking a loss.

mean making a profit. If the option's premium has decreased, closing out would mean cutting your losses and offsetting at least part of what you paid.

IMPORTANCE OF TIMING

The profit or loss you'll face at exit depends on whether your option is in-the-money, at-the-money, or out-of-the-money. Since the intrinsic value can change quickly, timing is very important for the options investor. Just a one dollar change in the price of the underlying stock might be the difference between a position that's profitable to hold, and one that you'll want to close

out. Especially as expiration nears, and time value drops quickly, you should monitor your positions in case they pass your predetermined point for exercise or for closing out. Time decay may work for or against you as the option gets closer to expiration, depending on the status of your option.

Another important timing factor is the exercise cut-off your brokerage firm imposes before expiration. This means you can't wait until the last minute to decide whether to exercise your option or close out a position. Check with your broker ahead of time to determine the firm's trading and exercise deadlines.

AT-THE-MONEY

If the stock price is between $90 and $92

- The option is in-the-money—or at-the-money, if the stock is exactly $90—but exercising it and then selling the shares won't provide enough profit to offset the cost of the premium. If you want to own the LMN shares, exercising it allows you to purchase them, and you might gain back your $200 in the future, if the stock rises.
- You can sell the option, hoping to earn back some of the premium you paid.
- You can let the option expire, losing $200. This may be the most costly exit, in this case.

AT-THE-MONEY

If the stock price is between $88 and $90

- The option is in-the-money—or at-the-money if the stock price is exactly $90—and might be exercised at the discretion of the put holder. You'll have to buy the shares at $90, but the premium reduces your net price paid to $88 a share, so you could still sell them on the market for a small profit.
- You could buy the option back, and you may or may not have to pay as much as you received for it.
- The option could expire unexercised if it is at-the-money, in which case the $200 would remain your profit.

OUT-OF-THE-MONEY

If the stock price is less than $90

- The option is out-of-the-money, and exercising it would mean purchasing shares at more than their market value. You'd lose money on top of what you spent on the premium.
- If there is any time value left, you can sell the option to partially offset what you paid for it.

OUT-OF-THE-MONEY

If the stock price is above $90

- The option is out-of-the-money, and most likely will not be exercised. You keep the $200 as your profit.

EXIT STRATEGIES

Rolling Up, Over, and Out

If you don't want to exit, you can roll into another options series.

If you've been successfully earning income by writing covered calls and would like to extend that strategy over time, or if your options strategy hasn't worked out as you planned but you think your initial forecast still holds true, you might consider **rolling** your options.

Rolling means first closing out an existing position, either by buying back the option you sold, or selling the option you bought. Next, you open a new position identical to the old option but with a new strike price, new expiration date, or both. If you are long an option, and you roll with enough time remaining before expiration, your old option will have some time premium left, which means it's likely that you can earn back some of what you paid. But on the opposite side, if you write a covered call, rolling might reduce your profit from the initial transaction. But you might roll anyway, if you don't want your stock called away from you.

ROLLING UP

If the new position you open has the same expiration date but a higher strike price, you're **rolling up**. You might roll up if you've written a covered call on a stock that has increased in price, and you'd like to maintain your short options position—or continue to generate income—without having your stock called away from you. Rolling up also appeals to call holders who have a more bullish market forecast on the underlying stock.

For example, say you think that EFG, a stock that's trading at $16, will increase in price in the next few months.

You buy a call with a strike price of $15, for a premium of $200.

As expiration nears, EFG has risen and is trading at $19. Your call is now worth $550. But you think EFG will continue to rise, so you decide to roll your call up.

$550	Received from sale of long call
− $200	Purchase of call
= $350	Profit

You purchase a new 20 call with a later expiration, paying $300. You earned $350 by closing out the older call, a profit that offsets the cost of the new call, leaving you with a net credit of $50 on the transaction.

$350	Profit from existing call
− $300	Purchase of new call
= $50	Net profit of rolling up

WHEN TO ROLL

Deciding when to roll an options position depends on several factors, including the costs involved, and your market prediction.

- As a covered call writer, you might roll down or out to extend your successful strategy and maintain the income provided by the premiums you receive

- If you use long puts to hedge your investment, rolling your options to ones with later expirations may extend the insurance they provide

- You might also consider rolling if a strategy you chose hasn't been successful, but you think that your prediction for a stock's movement is applicable for the coming months

ROLLING DOWN

If the new position you open has the same expiration but a lower strike price, you're **rolling down**. This strategy might appeal to investors who'd like to receive income from writing calls on a stock for which they have a long-term neutral prediction.

For example, say you write a covered call on stock JKL.

You predict it will be neutral or fall slightly below its current trading price of $74, so you write an 80 call, and receive $250 in premium. As expiration nears, the stock price has fallen to $72, and your short call is still out-of-the-money. That means it will likely expire unexercised, leaving you a $250 profit. But you think the stock will remain neutral or fall in the next few months, and would like to repeat your profitable trade.

You buy back the option you sold for $50, locking in a profit of $200. You then sell a 75 call and receive $150 in premium.

	$250	Received from long call
−	$50	Purchase of call
=	$200	Profit
+	$150	Received from new long call
=	$350	Total cash plus profit from rolling down

When rolling down a covered call, it's important to keep an eye on the price you paid when you initially bought the stock. If the market price falls near your original cost, it may make sense to consider closing out your position and selling the stock. But, if the price has fallen below your initial cost but begins to rise, you might have to scramble and buy back your call.

ROLLING OUT

If the new position you open has the same strike but a later expiration date, you're **rolling out**. If your options strategy hasn't yet been successful but you think you need more time for it to work, or if it has been successful and you think it will continue to be in the future, you might roll out.

For example, say you purchased 100 shares of LMN stock for $44 a share.

At the same time, you purchased a protective 40 LMN put to prevent losses of more than $4 a share. You paid $100 for the protection.

As expiration nears, LMN is trading at $45, but you still think there's a chance it will fall below $40 in the coming months. You sell your out-of-the-money put for $50, earning back some of what you paid for it.

You purchase a new 40 LMN put with a later expiration for $100, and extend your downside protection at a net cost of $150.

	−$100	Purchase put
+	$50	Received from put
=	−$50	
	−$100	Purchase of new put
=	−$150	Total cost

Index Options

You can balance your portfolio by investing in options on a stock index, which tracks an entire market or sector.

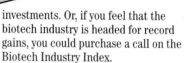

Index options are puts and calls on a stock index, rather than on an individual stock. For many investors, the appeal of index options is the exposure they provide to the performance of a group of stocks. Holding the equivalent stock positions of one index option—say the 500 stocks in the S&P 500—would require much more capital and numerous transactions.

Another attraction is that index options can be flexible, fitting into the financial plans of both conservative and more aggressive investors. If you've concentrated your portfolio on large US companies, you might sell options on an index that correlates to your portfolio to hedge your investments. Or, if you feel that the biotech industry is headed for record gains, you could purchase a call on the Biotech Industry Index.

Most index options are European style, which means they can only be exercised at expiration, not before.

HEDGING YOUR PORTFOLIO

Conservative investors may use index options to hedge their portfolios. If your portfolio drops in value, an index that corresponds to the movement of your portfolio will drop as well. By purchasing a put on that index, you're entitled, at expiration, to an amount of cash proportionate to the drop of the index below the strike price.

For example, say you have $100,000 invested in a portfolio that contains some of the larger stocks in the broad-based XYZ Index, which is currently trading at about 950. You'd like to protect yourself against a loss of more than 5%, or $5,000. You purchase a 900 put on the XYZ Index.

In the next few months, your portfolio drops in value by about 10%, to $90,000. Since XYZ has a similar makeup, it has also dropped by a little more than 10%, to 850. Your put is now in-the-money by 50 points, and at expiration you receive $5,000 minus the premium you paid for the put and any sales charges. Your overall loss is reduced to about $5,000, or 5%, which was your predetermined acceptable level. Keep in mind, though, that what you pay for the put affects your return.

If the index doesn't drop before expiration, your option will remain out-of-the-money or at-the-money. You can decide whether to extend your insurance by buying another option with a later expiration, or **rolling out**.

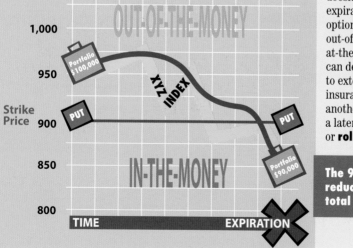

1,050

1,000

OUT-OF-THE-MONEY

950 — Portfolio $100,000

XYZ INDEX

Strike Price 900 — PUT — PUT

850 — IN-THE-MONEY — Portfolio $90,000

800

TIME — EXPIRATION

The 900 put reduces the total loss by 5%

USING LEVERAGE

Index options also appeal to investors because of the leverage they provide. Investors can participate in moves for a fraction of the cost of purchasing the equivalent assortment of stocks. And even a small change can result in large percentage gains. The downside of leverage, of course, is that if the market moves against expectations, the percentage loss can be high, and might be all of your investment.

The leverage of index options also means that if you're confident a certain sector is going to make gains, but you don't know which individual stock will rise, you can purchase an index call to benefit from the broader market shift.

WHAT'S THE RISK?

The risk of buying index options is the same as the risk of buying stock options: It's limited to the amount of premium you pay. If you're considering buying a put, it's important to weigh the cost of insuring your portfolio against the benefits of the insurance.

Index options writers, however, face substantial potential risk. Since the value of the index might drop suddenly, a put writer might owe a lot of cash. The same risk applies to a call writer, if the index increases sharply. And index call writers usually can't cover themselves by holding the underlying instrument, as they can with individual stock options.

MARGIN CONSIDERATIONS

The margin requirements are different for writing index options than for writing options on individual equities. In general, you initially need to deposit the entire premium, and at least 15% of the contract's **aggregate value**, or the level of the index multiplied by $100, in your margin account. Since the aggregate

HOW MUCH INSURANCE?

If you're using index puts to hedge your portfolio, you'll have to calculate the number of contracts to purchase in order to match the size of your portfolio.

1 Determine the current aggregate value of the index option:

_____	Current index value
x $100	
= _____	Aggregate value

2 Divide the value of your portfolio by the aggregate value.

_____	Your portfolio's value
÷ _____	Aggregate value from above
= _____	

The result is the number of contracts that will protect your entire portfolio.

Once you've determined the number of contracts that will cover your portfolio, you should calculate how much downside protection you want. The strike price you choose should match that amount, so that the insurance will kick in if the index drops that far. For example, if you want to protect against a decline greater than 10% in your portfolio, your strike price should be 90% of the current value of the index, which would be the value of the index if it drops 10% from current value.

value of an index option changes daily, the amount of the margin maintenance requirement fluctuates, which means you'll need to pay close attention to your account to avoid a margin call.

If your goal is to hedge your portfolio with index puts, the key is to find an index that mirrors the movement of your portfolio. Otherwise, what happens to the index won't accurately reflect what happens to your portfolio, and you may not offset any of its declining value. The first step is to find indexes that cover the same market or sector as your portfolio. Once you've narrowed your choices, you might use the past performance of an index or judge its volatility to find one that closely mirrors your portfolio's movement. But unless your portfolio exactly matches the makeup of an index—which is very unlikely—you'll always face the risk that it won't move the same way your portfolio does.

Tax Considerations

You can't ignore the tax implications of trading options.

Capital gains you realize on investments you sell—whether they're stocks, bonds, or options—are taxable unless you own them in a tax-deferred account or they're offset by capital losses. The rate at which those gains are taxed depends on how long you own the investment before you sell. The **long-term** capital gains rate applies to investments you've held for longer than a year. Through 2008, that rate is 15% for taxpayers whose regular bracket is 25% or higher. Taxpayers in the 10% or 15% tax bracket face only a 5% tax on their long-term gains.

The **short-term** rate applies to investments held less than a year. Any gains you realize on those investments will be taxed at your regular income tax rate, which may be significantly higher than the long-term gains rate. Most options transactions fall under the short-term category.

Any capital gains tax you pay is based on your overall gains for the year, which means that if you make a profit on one short-term investment, but lose money on another short-term investment, you can use that capital loss to offset all or part of your capital gain, reducing the amount of tax you'll pay. The same is true for long-term gains and losses. And for options, the premium and transaction costs are factored in to your gain or loss.

TAXING INDEXES

For certain index options, the rules are a little different. The IRS considers broad-based index options—such as the DJIA or the S&P 500—to be nonequity options, and you'll have to report them on a different form when you complete your tax return. All broad-based index options are subject to the **60/40 rule**, which means that 60% of your gain or loss is taxed at the long-term rate, and 40% is taxed at the short-term rate.

Additionally, if you have an open position in a broad-based index option at the year's end, you're required to **mark to market**, or calculate the option's value as if you sold it on the last business day of the year. You then include that unrealized gain or loss in your tax filings—even if you continue to hold the option into the next tax year. When you do close out the

WHAT'S THE TERM?
For stocks, calculating whether you've held an asset for more than a year or less than a year is a simple matter of comparing the purchase date to the sale date.

For long options positions, the rules are similar.
If an option you hold expires or you close it out, the amount of time you held the option determines whether your gain or loss is short term or long term.

For short positions, however, the matter is a bit more complex.

- If your short position expires unexercised, the premium you receive is a short-term gain, regardless of how long the position existed. This premium is taxable in the calendar year the option expires, which might not be the year you receive the premium. That means you might have more than a year to enjoy your profit without paying taxes on it.

  - If you close out your short position, your gain or loss is short term.

  - If you are assigned on your short option, the term of the gain or loss depends on a number of items. You should consult your tax adviser and review the *Taxes and Investing* booklet at www.888options.com.

For more detailed information, you can download a free booklet called *Taxes and Investing* from OIC's website, www.888options.com.

THE FORMS TO USE

Schedule D. The form on which you tally your capital gains and losses, and qualify them as short term or long term

SCHEDULE D
(Form 1040)
Department of the Treasury
Internal Revenue Service   (99)
Name(s) shown on Form 1040

Form 6781. The form on which you list nonequity options that are subject to the 60/40 rule or the mark to market requirement

Form **6781**
Department of the Treasury
Internal Revenue Service
Name(s) shown on tax return
Check all applicable boxes (see instructions)

Gains and
Co

position, you'll be taxed on any gain or loss realized from the beginning of the tax year, not from the opening of the position.

Options on market or sector indexes that are narrow-based are not subject to the 60/40 rule or the mark to market requirement. Instead, gains and losses are calculated and taxed in the same way as equity options.

KEEP GOOD RECORDS

You're required to report all options transactions, whether you realize a gain or loss, to the IRS. When it comes time to calculate your taxes, it will be easier if you have a written record of all the positions you opened and closed over the past year. That includes any confirmations or receipts you receive that detail the premium paid or received, transaction costs, the date the position was opened, when and how it was closed, and any gain or loss produced. You should also hold onto any account statements you receive from your brokerage firm. Most experts

recommend that you keep these documents for three years after you file, which is the normal time limit for the IRS to audit your return.

WORKING WITH A TAX ADVISER

Many options investors work with professional tax advisers when calculating their tax returns and when considering opening or closing options positions. Since exercising an option often involves a transfer of stock, options have tax consequences not only for your stock portfolio, but your larger financial situation as well.

For example, a tax adviser can help determine whether it might be beneficial to close out a covered call you wrote if you'd face a short-term gain on that stock were it called away from you. Or she might point out when you might be able to use losses to offset capital gains. While you don't want to make investment decisions solely because of their tax implications, neither do you want to ignore the impact taxes can have on your bottom line.

A tax adviser will also help you understand the IRS rules as they apply to your options positions, and will be able to explain the often complex rules that apply to certain options strategies, such as straddles.

ADVISER

MY RECORDS

If you've written covered calls, it's important to pay attention to how you report the transaction on your tax return. You might sell a call in November of one year, and buy it back in January of the next. That means your sale date comes before your buy date, which is the opposite of most investments. If you get confused, you might make an error on your tax return, so be sure to keep good records and double-check the forms before you submit them.

Trading Options

When you're choosing a brokerage firm, consider the tools and the expertise at your disposal.

There have been some major changes in equity options investing since the mid-1990s. Thanks to the Internet, you have easier access to a wide range of timely information that allows you to research underlying investments on which options are available, track real-time or near real-time prices changes, and follow trading activity in contracts that interest you.

You also have a broader selection of brokerage firms to handle your orders. They range from traditional full-service firms to discount firms that operate exclusively online. Some firms specialize in options, while others offer options accounts in addition to regular brokerage accounts. If you choose an online firm or an online account with a traditional firm, you should ask how you'd trade if the Internet connection isn't working. Many firms offer phone service, though it may cost more to trade that way.

COMPARATIVE TOOLS

In order to be competitive, many brokerage firms offer their customers advanced tools and technology to help them research and track securities and strategies. You might have access to some or all of the following tools through your firm's website:

Options calculator. If you enter the details of a particular options trade, this electronic tool can calculate the potential profit and loss of adopting the strategy, as well as your breakeven point and any margin requirement. An options calculator can also be used to determine **the Greeks** for a particular option and the annualized returns for various strategies, which allows you to compare options strategies with different time periods.

EXECUTING A TRADE

Depending on the firm you use, you'll find differences in the cost of trading and your access to professional advice. But whether you enter your options trading order yourself using your online account or you telephone your order to your broker, you put the same process in motion.

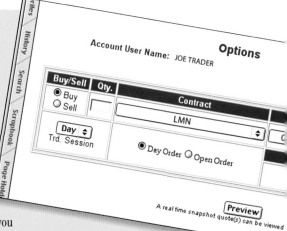

1 In order to initiate a trade, you provide the details of your trade, which include:

- The symbol of the option or the underlying stock
- Whether you're buying to open, buying to close, selling to open, or selling to close
- Whether you want a put or call
- The strike price
- The expiration month
- A specific buy or sell price, or a market order to buy or sell at the current market price
- Whether you'd like to use a cash account or a margin account
- With some brokers, you can request a multi-part transaction, such as a spread

2 The next step is confirming your order before it is placed, double-checking the information displayed online or repeated back to you by your broker to make sure it's correct.

3 After submitting the order, you should receive a confirmation that it has been placed—but not yet executed. There may be a lapse between when your order is placed and when your brokerage firm can fill it. Some firms' websites offer an order status page, where you can view your executed orders and any current, pending orders.

Options screener. You can find specific options that match a strategy, a particular market forecast, or other condition. For example, if you were looking for options with a very high implied volatility, an options screener would provide a list of options with the highest implied volatility.

Options chains. If you select a particular stock or stock index, you can see a chart of all put and call series offered on it, the delayed or real-time premiums, and other characteristics such as volume and open interest.

Options information. You can research options, finding out about underlying stocks and stock indexes, as well as price history, volatility, and other data.

SPECIAL CONSIDERATIONS

If you're just beginning to trade options, you may want to work with an experienced investment adviser at a full-service firm who can advise you on the options strategies or the specific contracts that

Order

Account Number: 022049000

nth/Year	Strike	Put/Call
◆ 2005 ◆	45	● Put
		○ Call

ice	Order Type	Open/Close
	Market ◆	● Open Pos.
		○ Close Pos.

[Clear]

Order Preview page.

4 When your option order has been executed—it may be a matter of minutes or several hours, depending on the type of order—you should receive a notification that will include the price at which it was executed. Because most options are not traded as heavily as most stocks, execution can take longer.

5 You can monitor the status of your options positions through your brokerage firm's website.

may be most appropriate for you. Or, if you'd prefer to trade on your own, you may want to choose an online firm.

The first step is often to ask your other professional advisers, friends, or colleagues who trade options for referrals. You can check the OIC website, www.888options.com, for a list of firms, and you can use the SEC's EDGAR database (www.sec.gov/edgar.shtml) to search for information and regulatory filings on any firm. If you've already opened an account with a brokerage firm but you're not satisfied with the tools they offer or the execution of your orders, shop around.

You can find reviews of brokerage firms in financial publications, and some firms' websites allow you trial access to their account holder services. You may also want to compare the range of services offered by several firms. For example, some brokerage firms offer a wide variety of educational information, and others have more experience executing complex transactions.

THE LANGUAGE OF ORDERS

There are ways to restrict an order you place if you'd like it to be executed only at a certain price, for example, or within a specific period of time. A **limit order** restricts the transaction to the highest price you're willing to pay if you're purchasing, or the lowest price you're willing to accept if you're selling. As with stock orders, if the market has passed your buy limit, your order will not be filled. The opposite of a limit order is a **market order**, which means you're willing to pay whatever the market price is at the time your trade is entered.

Most orders are **day orders**, which means they will be automatically canceled if they're not filled by the end of the trading day. Alternatively, you might place a **good 'til canceled order (GTC)**, which means it is pending until your brokerage firm fills the order, unless you cancel it. Some brokerage firms have 90-day limits on GTC orders, so check with yours for their policy.

A **stop-loss order** is a request to automatically close your options position if its price moves beyond a certain predetermined level. Stop-loss orders are often used on stock transactions to stem losses if prices drop dramatically. Some brokerage firms allow stop-loss orders on options.

Options Information Sources

The smart approach is to prepare for trading by researching your options.

The key to smart investing is being well informed. As an options investor, this means you'll want to research the underlying stock for a particular options series, as well as the options class and the overall market. While this takes time and requires effort on your part, the good news is that the information you need is readily available through a variety of sources—and much of it is free.

LOOK ONLINE

Today, most options investors use the Internet as a source for at least some of their research. The Internet is easy to access for most people, much of the information is free, and news is almost always up-to-date, since financial websites are updated frequently. Even those investors who don't give their buy and sell orders online can research options and underlying stocks on the Internet.

COLLEAGUES AND FRIENDS

Don't neglect your personal connections and business contacts when researching investments. Discussing options and financial markets with colleagues and friends lets you compare other perspectives with your own. Someone else's investing experience might serve as a cautionary tale or introduce you to a particular investment or a certain market sector that you might not have investigated on your own. And if you know people who have been investing longer or more successfully than you have, you might be able to learn a lot from them. Don't forget, though, that a tip from an acquaintance is never a substitute for doing your own research. Ultimately, you're responsible for all of your investment choices.

- OIC's website, www.888options.com, and OCC's website, www.options clearing.com, both provide general options education, plus industry-wide volume, open interest, contract adjustments, SEC filings, and expiration cycles, among other topics.

- The websites of the options exchanges offer information on the options they list as well as real-time and delayed quotes, volume, and open interest.

- Both online and traditional full-service brokerage firms offer their clients website access to information about specific options and strategies, as well as analysis and recommendations.

- A range of commercial sites are exclusively devoted to options information. Most of these are accessible by paid subscription only, so you'll have to use your own judgment to decide whether their education and analysis is reliable and worth paying for.

- Many of the leading financial information sites offer substantial data as well. These sites are usually free, and include CBS MarketWatch (www.cbs.market watch.com) and Yahoo! Finance (http://finance. yahoo.com).

When using the Internet for research, it's important to be discriminating about the reliability of a source, just as you would when using any investment research. You can find a list of reputable options websites at www.888options.com. They might serve as good starting points for your research.

CHECK OUT THE PAPER?

Newspapers are another resource to consider, but the information they offer may not be as timely or as comprehensive as the news on the Internet. In the financial section of a newspaper, you may be able to find a summary of the previous day's options trading—including volume, open interest, and premiums—for some of the most popular options. If you're looking for information about a particular option, it might be

hard to find, since the space devoted to options in a newspaper is increasingly limited. But you can check online editions for recent articles. Financial newspapers are more likely than general newspapers to have options information.

If you're interested in learning about options but aren't ready to start trading, a daily scan of a newspaper's financial section can be a good way to see how the market moves, and familiarize yourself with the way options information is presented.

SUBSCRIBING TO NEWSLETTERS

Financial newsletters are another popular source of options information. Most options newsletters are paid services that offer subscribers a periodic update on options news, educational information, and specific recommendations on options and strategies. Some newsletters are printed, while others are only available online or delivered by email. Newsletters are usually written by options experts who offer their opinion and analysis—but who can't guarantee the success of any strategy. Some newsletters are tailored to the needs of specific groups of investors, so it's important to look for one that suits you, as well as one you trust to deliver accurate, reliable analysis.

PUT A BROKER TO WORK

If you already work with a brokerage firm, you might be able to find options information and analysis through their website or office, just as you might when researching a stock purchase. If your brokerage firm specializes in trading options, they are likely to have a greater wealth of resources for you. Even if the firm focuses primarily on stocks, you might be able to use their research on an option's underlying instrument. But it's a good idea to support that research with options-specific information.

If you're comfortable working with your broker for research and analysis on your other investments, it might make sense to do the same for options research as well. You should check first, however, to find out whether your broker has options trading experience.

A DISCRIMINATING READER

Newsletters and online columns often provide an analysis of options information and recommend specific trades and strategies based on that analysis. They can also be good places to learn more about individual benchmarks or indicators, and how to use them as the basis for creating strategies. If you subscribe to a newsletter or regularly read an online options column—and you consider it to be a trustworthy source of analysis—you can use their recommendations as a starting point. But you should always do your own independent research to see if the information you come across backs up any assertions or predictions they've made.

Applying Options Information and Analysis

Once you do your research, put it to work for your portfolio.

There's a wealth of information about trading options at your fingertips. But the sheer amount often seems overwhelming. So you need to know how to use that information to create options strategies.

USING BENCHMARKS

Benchmarks are measurements that you can use to judge the relative position of the security you're interested in, compared to the market. One benchmark many options investors use is the **CBOE Volatility Index**, which is commonly known by its ticker symbol, **VIX**. In the same way that stock indexes are compilations of stock prices, VIX is a compilation of the implied volatilities of S&P 500 index options. You can use VIX as a benchmark to measure how volatile investors feel the S&P 500 index—and by extension, the stock market—will be. In general, a higher volatility indicates a bearish market sentiment, though there are exceptions. And keep in mind, that's only how investors predict the market will behave. The actual market movement may or may not match predictions.

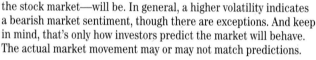

$$C = S_0 \Phi \left[\frac{\ln\{\frac{S_0}{K}\} + (r + \frac{1}{2}\sigma^2)\, n}{\sigma\sqrt{n}} \right] - Ke^{-rn} \Phi \left[\frac{\ln\{\frac{S_0}{K}\} + (r - \frac{1}{2}\sigma^2)\, n}{\sigma\sqrt{n}} \right]$$

PRICING MODELS

Another benchmark you can use to analyze options is an options pricing model that estimates the theoretical fair value for a given options position.

In 1973, three mathematicians—Fischer Black, Myron Scholes, and Robert Merton—published their formula, known as the Black-Scholes model, for calculating the premium of an option, accounting for the variety of factors that affect premium. You can find the actual formula on many options websites, but what's most important to know are the variables that go into the formula. These are the variables affecting an option's premium:

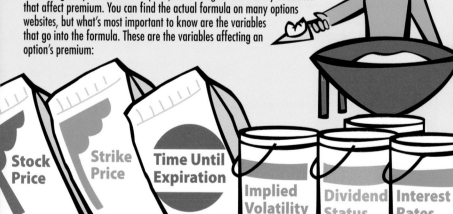

Stock Price **Strike Price** **Time Until Expiration** **Implied Volatility** **Dividend Status** **Interest Rates**

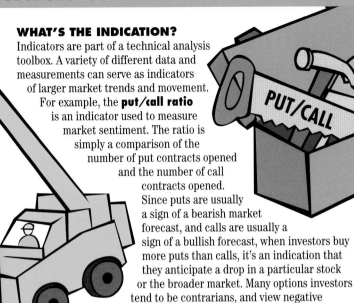

WHAT'S THE INDICATION?

Indicators are part of a technical analysis toolbox. A variety of different data and measurements can serve as indicators of larger market trends and movement. For example, the **put/call ratio** is an indicator used to measure market sentiment. The ratio is simply a comparison of the number of put contracts opened and the number of call contracts opened. Since puts are usually a sign of a bearish market forecast, and calls are usually a sign of a bullish forecast, when investors buy more puts than calls, it's an indication that they anticipate a drop in a particular stock or the broader market. Many options investors tend to be contrarians, and view negative market sentiment as a buying opportunity.

BE CONSISTENT

Whatever benchmark, indicator, or analysis you rely on to shape your options strategies, it's important that you determine which information is important to you. If you choose one or two pieces of data as indicators or benchmarks, be consistent and stick with them over the long term. That way, you can easily track the small number you've chosen, rather than being overwhelmed by trying to follow every piece of market data available.

Consistency is also important when you're evaluating your options positions. Say you bought an option because your research and calculations indicated it was undervalued, and you think its premium will go up. But you've recently looked at the put/call ratio, and you're worried that the market is about to dip.

You could close out your position, but if you believe the option is still under-priced, you'll forfeit the whole strategy, which might have proved successful. Instead, when you buy or write an option, you should have a plan in place for evaluating whether to close the position, based on the same benchmark or indicator that prompted you to open the position. If you're consistent in how you evaluate positions, you'll be more confident when deciding whether to hold a position, or exit and cut your losses.

The Black-Scholes formula, though perhaps the best known, isn't the only method for computing an option's theoretical value. Equity options are typically priced using either the Cox-Ross-Rubenstein model, which was developed in 1979 for American-style options that allow early exercise, or the Whaley model. Inputs to any of these models can be tweaked, or manually adjusted, to illustrate the impact of stock movement, volatility changes, or other factors that may influence an option's actual value. For example, you could adjust the quantities of a potential spread to see how that change would affect the delta, gamma, and other Greeks.

The limitation of all pricing models is that actual premiums are determined by market forces, not by formula—no matter how sophisticated that formula might be. Market influences can actually result in highly unexpected price behavior during the life of a given options contract.

But while no model can reliably predict what options premiums will be available to you or other investors at some point in the future, some investors do use pricing models to anticipate an option's premium under certain future circumstances. For instance, you can calculate how an option might react to an interest rate increase or a dividend distribution to help you better predict the outcomes of your options strategies.

Reading Options Charts

Options tables look a lot like stock tables, but there are important distinctions.

If you research options in a newspaper, you'll need to be familiar with options charts, which list information and statistics from the previous trading day. The options information you'll find in newspapers isn't as comprehensive as what's available online, since only the most active options are listed, but newspapers may still be a good resource for an overall view of the market.

Calls are listed separately from puts. Some days only a call or a put will trade for a particular stock or index. In that case, an ellipsis (…) appears in that column, as it does for the Hatchery August 35 puts.

NEWSPAPER OPTIONS TABLES

A list of options beginning with the closest **expiration date** and lowest **strike price** appears after the name of the underlying instrument. Often, the same month appears several times with different strike prices, but with the groupings by price rather than date. For example, since JK Industries has options at 40 and 42.50, the 40s are listed first, followed by the 42.50s.

OPTION/STRIKE	EXP	-CALL- VOL	LAST	-PUT- VOL	LAST
Dave Co 7.50	Jan	3772	1.20	3266	0.90
Htchry 35	Aug	5000	1	…	
35.89 35	Sep	5074	1.30	105	0.65
JkIn 40	Aug	1108	0.70	3565	0.40
40.35 42.50	Aug	4243	0.05	226	2.20
40.35 42.50	Sep	5204	0.75	193	3.30
Lumn 7.50	Sep	220	3.50	8718	0.95
Msm Th 42.50	Sep	3294	3.70	927	1
44.85 45	Aug	6411	0.60	612	0.75
44.85 45	Sep	4330	2	196	2.15
New Mn 17.50	Aug	5181	1.50	1701	0.05
19.07 19	Aug	6708	0.30	4674	0.25
19.07 20	Aug	973	0.05	3785	1
19.07 20	Sep	2981	0.65	1345	1.60
Snchz 17.50	Aug	8151	0.50	105	0.05
18.14 17.50	Sep	8027	0.90	35	0.40
Xerxs 80	Aug	5211	0.90	497	0.25
80.79 80	Sep	4241	1.95	271	1.80

The **name of the underlying stock** is listed in bold. Some names are easy to recognize. Other companies are referred to by abbreviations, sometimes the same ones used in stock tables and sometimes different ones. You can find the company's name using an Internet search engine.

The number in the first column below the option name is the most recent **market price** of the underlying stock. In this example, Xerxes traded at $80.79 at the end of the previous trading day.

Information about the most actively traded options and LEAPS is given separately, often at the beginning or end of the options columns.

Volume reports the number of trades during the previous trading day. The number is unofficial, but gives a sense of the activity in each option. Often, you'll notice that trading increases as the expiration date gets closer. But many factors contribute to trading volume, and expiration date is just one influence.

Last is the previous trading day's closing price for the option. In this case, the Sanchez 17.50 September call closed at 90 cents, or $90 for an option on 100 shares at $17.50.

PROFIT AND LOSS CHARTS

As you compare different options strategies, you will probably encounter a standard chart for each strategy, meant to help you visualize the potential profit or loss you'd face under different circum-stances, and the point at which you'd break even. These charts are available at options websites and through brokerage firms. The following chart illustrates the profit and loss a call holder faces.

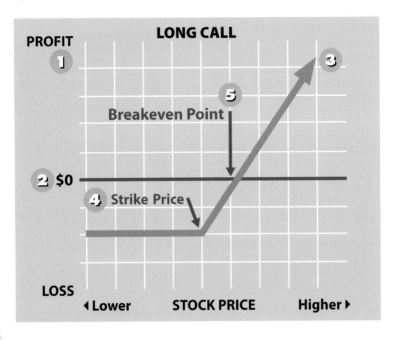

The vertical axis shows the scale of profit and loss, measured in dollars. The center of this axis is a breakeven line, where your profit or loss is $0.

The horizontal axis, shown in red, shows the price of the underlying stock: The farther to the right, the higher the stock price.

The blue arrow tracks the profit or loss you'd realize at a particular stock price. If you pick a stock price on the horizontal axis, and find the height of the arrow at that stock price, you'll have an idea of your profit—or loss. In this case, the loss is steady, or flat, for all stock prices below the strike price. The loss decreases as the stock price rises above the strike price—but you don't realize a profit until the stock price moves past the breakeven point.

The **strike price** you choose determines where the profit and loss line bends, since if the stock is below that price you'll face a loss. Above that price your loss drops until you begin to realize a profit.

Your **breakeven point** is the stock price at which you'll neither lose money nor make a profit on the investment. With a long call, the break-even point is to the right of—or higher than—the option's strike price. Since this strategy calls for spending money to purchase the option, you'll have to earn back the premium before you can realize a profit. If this chart were for call writing, your breakeven point would be to the left of—or lower than—the strike price, since premium received would partially offset loss.

USE 'EM OR LOSE 'EM?

While it's possible to graph a profit and loss chart using the numbers from a specific pur-chase or sale you're considering, many investors use generic profit and loss charts to get an overview of what will happen as the underlying stock price increases or decreases. If you'd like to be able to visualize your strategies, this tool might be helpful. You can find profit and loss charts for each of the basic options strategies on the OIC website, www.888options.com. What a chart can help clarify is whether a strategy's potential for gain or loss is limited, as it is with a spread, or unlimited, as with long or short calls.

Options Chains

Learn how to translate the specialized options tools you can find online.

Instead of options tables, many websites offer **options chains** or **options strings**. You select a particular underlying instrument, and can see a chain of all the options currently available, so that you can compare the prices for calls and puts, different strike prices, and different expiration months.

The Options Industry Council

1-888-OPTIONS

Reg

Some options quoting software gives you the choice of seeing the Greeks for a particular options class, or to view only LEAPS on that class.

Show me All

2 months

☐ Please also include strike prices from
☐ Just show me the LEAPS.
☐ Just give me the Greeks (theoretical

To avoid long download times please try lim necessary Calls or Puts; especially when vie

The top horizontal line displays information about the underlying stock, the previous day's closing price, and the current opening price.

XERXES & YUMAN (XY)

Symbol	Last	Time	N
XY	93.95	10:44	-0

Ticker lists the ticker symbol for an options series. The last two letters indicate the expiration month and strike price.

Last is the most recent trading price for the option. The last options price reported online is usually updated several times an hour if trading is active, as opposed to once a day, as is the case with newspaper options charts. The last price for the October 50 call was 42.50, or $4,250 a contract.

			Calls	
Ticker	Last	Net	Bid	Ask
XY JJ	42.50	0.00	43.90	44.10
XY JK	37.50	0.00	38.90	39.10
XY JL	28.60	0.00	33.90	34.10
XY JM	26.70	0.00	28.90	29.10

BID AND ASK

The bid is the price that a buyer is willing to pay for an option, and the ask is the price that a seller is willing to accept. In general, the two prices are slightly different, and the gap between them is known as the spread. So how does that affect individual investors?

When you buy or sell an option—or a stock—you're likely buying from and selling to a market maker. The market makers ensure that the marketplace is liquid, or that options can be easily bought and sold. In return for providing this service, market makers bid slightly lower when buying and ask slightly higher when selling. They may make a profit of only a few cents on a contract, but they trade in high volume every day, so the small profits add up.

As a rule of thumb, the more actively traded an option is, the smaller the spread will be. That's because more than one market maker will be competing to trade that options series. By checking the bid and ask columns, and comparing them with volume, you can get a picture of the market activity for a particular option. And because several exchanges trade many of the most popular options, the bid and ask can vary from exchange to exchange. Options brokers focus on getting the best execution price from any of these exchanges.

You can choose whether to display all options strike prices, or only those that are in-the-money or close to being in-the-money.

The date indicates the expiration month. The left-hand column displays October calls, and the right-hand column shows October puts.

The bold numbers indicate the most recent market price for the underlying stock, and the net gain or loss from its opening price. Some websites offer real-time price quotes, while others show delayed quotes.

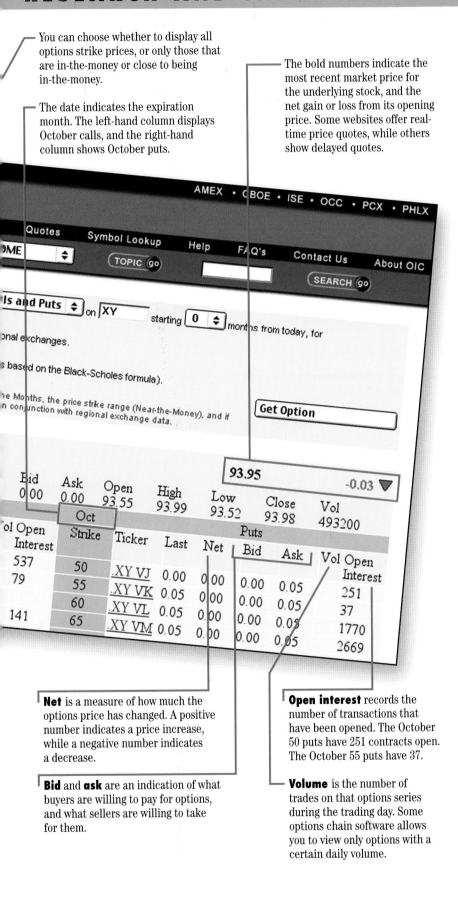

AMEX • CBOE • ISE • OCC • PCX • PHLX

Quotes Symbol Lookup Help FAQ's Contact Us About OIC

OME [◆] (TOPIC go) [   ] Contact Us About OIC

(SEARCH go)

Is and Puts [◆] on [XY   ] starting [0 ◆] months from today, for

onal exchanges.

s based on the Black-Scholes formula).

he Months, the price strike range (Near-the-Money), and if n conjunction with regional exchange data.

Get Option

93.95   -0.03 ▼

Bid	Ask	Open	High	Low	Close	Vol
0.00	0.00	93.55	93.99	93.52	93.98	493200

ol Open Interest	Oct Strike	Ticker	Last	Net	Puts Bid	Ask	Vol Open Interest
537	50	.XY VJ	0.00	0.00	0.00	0.05	251
79	55	.XY VK	0.05	0.00	0.00	0.05	37
	60	.XY VL	0.05	0.00	0.00	0.05	1770
141	65	.XY VM	0.05	0.00	0.00	0.05	2669

Net is a measure of how much the options price has changed. A positive number indicates a price increase, while a negative number indicates a decrease.

Bid and **ask** are an indication of what buyers are willing to pay for options, and what sellers are willing to take for them.

Open interest records the number of transactions that have been opened. The October 50 puts have 251 contracts open. The October 55 puts have 37.

Volume is the number of trades on that options series during the trading day. Some options chain software allows you to view only options with a certain daily volume.

Options Symbols and Sources

Instead of writing out the name of the underlying stock and the strike and expiration date of the option, many online sources use a shorthand symbol that expresses all those characteristics. These are generally the ticker symbols investors use when trading an option.

DECODING SYMBOLS

Every options series has its own particular symbol of three, four, or five letters. Since some options information may use options symbols to save space, you'll need to be able to decode them. It's easy, once you break a symbol down into its elements. Say you come across a premium for XYZRK.

The standard symbol format is:

Options root symbol

XYZ R K—Strike price

Expiration month and type (call or put)

Symbol. In some cases, the options root symbol is the same as the underlying stock symbol, but it may also be different. It will vary if the stock symbol has four letters, for example, since options roots never have more than three letters. If you look up XYZ, you'll find it refers to options on XYZ stock. LEAPS have different root symbols, which change into the standard symbols within 10 to 12 months of expiration. You can find the options symbol for a particular stock through the OIC website, at www.888options.com.

Strike. In the same way, each strike price is assigned a letter. Since the strike price could be as low as $5 or as high as $300, a letter indicates only the last two digits of the strike price. **A** represents a $5 strike, as well as a $105 strike and a $205 strike. Since XYZ is currently trading at $40, you can tell that the **K** means the strike price is $55, which is the **K** value closest to $40.

So **XYZRK** is an XYZ June 55 put.

A	5	105	205	305
B	10	110	210	310
C	15	115	215	315
D	20	120	220	320
E	25	125	225	325
F	30	130	230	330
G	35	135	235	335
H	40	140	240	340
I	45	145	245	345
J	50	150	250	350
K	55	155	255	355
L	60	160	260	360
M	65	165	265	365
N	70	170	270	370
O	75	175	275	375
P	80	180	280	380
Q	85	185	285	385
R	90	190	290	390
S	95	195	295	395
T	100	200	300	400
U	7.5	37.5	67.5	97.5
V	12.5	42.5	72.5	102.5
W	17.5	47.5	77.5	107.5
X	22.5	52.5	82.5	112.5
Y	27.5	57.5	87.5	117.5
Z	32.5	62.5	92.5	122.5

Month	Call	Put
January	A	M
February	B	N
March	C	O
April	D	P
May	E	Q
June	F	R
July	G	S
August	H	T
September	I	U
October	J	V
November	K	W
December	L	X

Month. Each expiration month is assigned two letters: one for calls that expire in that month, and a different letter for puts.

The R, therefore, means you're looking at a put on XYZ that expires in June.

In some cases, stock prices fluctuate so widely that options may be listed for the same underlying stock with strike prices $100 or more apart. In order to avoid confusion, new root symbols called **overflow** or **wrap** symbols are created. For stock XYZ, there might be a wrap symbol of WYZ that designates those options with strikes of $105 and higher. So WYZRK would be an XYZ June 155 put.

INDUSTRY ORGANIZATIONS

The Options Industry Council (OIC) and The Options Clearing Corporation (OCC)

One North Wacker Drive, Suite 500
Chicago, IL 60606
Email: options@theocc.com
Toll-free: 888-OPTIONS (888-678-4667)

You can call OIC and OCC toll-free to speak with experienced representatives. While they don't provide investment advice, they can answer options-related questions you might have—whether about the basics of options trading or about a specific, advanced strategy.

OIC website

www.888options.com

Learn about options and strategies, find free educational seminars near you, and get the latest news on options trading at the OIC website.

- Take online classes on options trading
- OIC offers a printable online glossary defining all of the terms commonly used in options trading

OCC website

www.optionsclearing.com

On the OCC website, you can find educational tools and volume information, as well as options pricing calculators and a database of all listed options.

You can view an options symbol directory, new listings, and contract adjustment memos.

NASD

www.nasd.com

You can find resources about a variety of securities on the website of the association of securities dealers, which includes all US brokerage firms.

- Find tips for protecting your investments and avoiding fraud
- Learn about the markets and other educational topics
- You can also use the NASD website to check the background of a brokerage firm or investment adviser you're considering

Securities and Exchange Commission (SEC)

www.sec.gov

The SEC is a government agency that regulates the securities industry and protects individual investors.

You can also research individual companies using EDGAR, a database of the mandatory corporate reports and filings.

THE EXCHANGES

The exchange websites offer directories of all the options they list, as well as the latest trading data, delayed and real-time quotes, product specifications, and an expiration calendar for those options. The exchanges also provide market information for the stock, index, or other options that they list, and their official trading hours. You can also learn about the trading technology at each exchange.

In addition to the exchange-specific information, most of these websites offer visitors plenty of educational tools, including the latest options news, explanations of basic options information, and details about a variety of options strategies. You can also find profit and loss diagrams, stock charts, links to downloadable documents and brochures, and glossaries of options terms. The options exchanges' websites also offer answers to commonly asked questions and links to outside resources that might be helpful.

American Stock Exchange (AMEX)

86 Trinity Place
New York, NY 10006
Toll-free: 800-THE-AMEX (800-843-2639)
www.amex.com

Chicago Board Options Exchange (CBOE)

400 South LaSalle Street
Chicago, IL 60605
Toll-free: 877-THE-CBOE (877-843-2263)
www.cboe.com

International Securities Exchange (ISE)

60 Broad Street
New York, NY 10004
212-943-2400
www.iseoptions.com

Pacific Exchange (PCX)

301 Pine Street
San Francisco, CA 94104
Toll-free: 877-PCX-PCX1 (877-729-7291)
www.pacificex.com

Philadelphia Stock Exchange (PHLX)

1900 Market Street
Philadelphia, PA 19103
Toll-free: 800-THE-PHLX (800-843-7459)
www.phlx.com

Strategy Screener

You can screen for strategies based on your risk tolerance and market forecast.

As you consider whether to add equity options to your investment portfolio, you might find it helpful to review these strategy screeners. First, if you've identified an objective you're trying to achieve—to hedge a stock position, for example, or receive income—look at the corresponding table. Next, choose the level of risk that you're willing to take. If you're new to options, you'll probably want to choose a low-risk strategy to begin with. Finally, find a forecast that fits your expectations, from very bearish to very bullish, either on an individual stock, or on the market as a whole. You'll find a potential strategy that fits your particular situation and forecast.

These tables are far from comprehensive, but they can be helpful shortcuts to identifying an appropriate options strategy. Once you've begun considering a strategy, you'll have to do some research on your own to match it with an underlying security that might work to meet your objective.

EXPIRATION CYCLES

If you're considering opening an options position on a particular stock, you'll always have the choice of contracts expiring in four different months. That's the easy part. What can be a little more complicated is figuring out which months those are.

That's because there are three factors at work:

1 Options are always available for the current month and the following one. So on January 1, you can buy or sell options that expire in January and in February on all stocks with listed options. On February 1, you can buy options expiring in February and March for all stocks—and so on through the year.

2 The two other months in which options on a specific stock expire are determined by the **expiration cycle** to which the underlying stock is assigned. There are three cycles, beginning in January, February, and March, each including four months, one in each calendar quarter. Stocks are assigned randomly to one of those cycles.

So, on January 1, options on a stock assigned to the January cycle would be available in April and July, the next two months in the cycle, as well as January and February. Those on a stock assigned to the February cycle would be available in May and August in addition to January and February. Stocks assigned to the March cycle would have options expiring in June and September.

Cycle 1 (January)	Cycle 2 (February)	Cycle 3 (March)
January	February	March
April	May	June
July	August	September
October	November	December

3 The current month's options expire on the Saturday following the third Friday, and a new options series with a new expiration is added on the following Monday. If, for example, January 20 were a Monday, new options series expiring in March would be added to the January and February cycles, and a new series expiring in September would be added for stocks in the March cycle.

If LEAPS are available on an options class, there might be five expiration months trading at a given time, in addition to the LEAPS, since LEAPS convert into regular options with a January expiration in the final year of the contract.

If you'd like to find out the available expirations for an option class you're considering, you can call 888-OPTIONS, or check on OIC's website, www.888options.com. You can also check the third and fourth expiration months of an options chain, which will tell you the cycle to which the underlying stock has been assigned.

	Your Risk Tolerance	Your Expectation	Possible Strategy*
SPECULATE OR RECEIVE INCOME	Low	Very bullish	Buy out-of-the-money calls
	Low	Bullish	Buy calls
	Low	Moderately bullish	Open bull call spread
	Low	Neutral or bullish	Open bull put spread
	Low	Neutral or bearish	Open bear call spread
	Low	Moderately bearish	Open bear put spread
	Low	Bearish	Buy puts
	Low	Very bearish	Buy out-of-the-money puts
	Moderate	Neutral to moderately bullish	Write covered calls on stock you own
	High	Neutral to bullish	Write naked puts
	Extremely high	Neutral to bearish	Write naked calls
IMPROVE YOUR PURCHASE PRICE OR PROTECT PROFITS	Low	Neutral to slightly bullish	Buy calls to lock in purchase price
	Low	Neutral to bullish	Buy-write to reduce your net price paid
	Low	Neutral, long-term bullish	Write puts to reduce your net price paid
	Low	Neutral to moderately bearish	Open a collar to lock in potential gains
	Low	Very bearish, long-term bullish	Buy puts
	Low	Bearish, long-term bullish	Buy out-of-the-money puts
PROFIT FROM A MARKET OR SECTOR MOVE	Low	Bullish	Buy index calls
	Low	Bearish	Buy index puts
	Extremely high	Neutral to bearish	Write index calls
	Extremely high	Neutral to bullish	Write index puts

* These strategies are described as possibilities, not recommendations. No strategy is guaranteed success, and you are responsible for doing adequate research and making your own investment choices.

American-style An option that you can exercise at any point before expiration. Equity options are American style.

Ask The price that market makers or sellers will accept to sell an option.

Assignment When an options holder exercises the contract, an options writer is chosen to fulfill the obligation.

At-the-money When the price of the underlying stock is the same as or close to your option's strike price.

Black-Scholes formula A pricing model that calculates the theoretical value of an option, based on factors including volatility and time until expiration.

Breakeven point The stock price at which, if you exercise your option, you would earn back your initial investment.

Buyer If you purchase an options contract, regardless of whether you're opening or closing a position, you're a buyer.

Buy-write You simultaneously purchase shares of stock and write a call on that stock.

Bid The price that market makers or buyers will accept to buy an option.

Call If you buy a call, you hold the right to purchase a certain security at the strike price, on or before the expiration date. If you write a call, you face an obligation to sell a certain security at the strike price, on or before the expiration date, if the call is exercised.

Cash-settled An option contract, usually an index option, that requires cash to change hands at exercise. The exact amount of cash is calculated by a specific formula, using the option's intrinsic value.

Close If you buy or sell an option in order to offset a position you previously opened, you're closing.

Collar You simultaneously purchase a protective put and write a covered call. Also known as a fence.

Covered call You write a call on stock you hold. Also known as an overwrite.

Day order An order you place to purchase an option that is canceled if it is not filled before the end of the trading day.

Equity option A contract to buy or sell shares of a stock, an exchange-traded fund (ETF), or other equity interest at a certain price before a certain time.

European-style An options contract that you can exercise only at expiration, not before.

Exercise If you're an options holder, exercise means you give an order to act on an option, and the options writer must transfer to you or receive from you the shares of stock—or amount of cash—covered by the option.

Expiration date The date after which an option is no longer valid, and you can no longer exercise it.

Fungible Able to be bought and sold on multiple exchanges or markets.

Good 'til canceled order (GTC) An order you place to purchase or sell an option that is valid until it is filled, you cancel it, or your brokerage firm's time limit on GTC orders expires.

Hedge An investment that's intended to limit or reduce potential losses on another investment by returning a profit under the opposite conditions.

Holder If you purchase an option to open a position, you're a holder.

In-the-money When the strike price of an option is below the market price for the underlying stock, in the case of a call, and above the underlying stock price, in the case of a put.

Intrinsic value The value of an option if you exercised it at a given moment. Out-of-the-money and at-the-money options have no intrinsic value. For in-the-money options, the intrinsic value is the difference between the strike price and the underlying stock price.

Leg Each separate options position in a strategy that calls for you to hold multiple positions at the same time, such as a spread.

Leverage If you leverage, you use a small amount of money to control an investment of much larger value.

Limit order An order you place to purchase or sell a security or financial instrument, such as an option, only at a certain price or better.

Long When you own a security or option. You might have a long position, or be long.

Long-term Equity AnticiPation Securities (LEAPS®) An option whose expiration date is between one and three years away.

Market order An order to purchase or sell an option at its current market price.

Mark to market This tax rule requires you to calculate the theoretical profit you'd earn on an asset if you sold it at the end of the tax year. You owe tax on that unrealized gain. This rule applies to broad-based index options.

Married put You simultaneously purchase shares of stock and a put on that stock.

Naked call You write a call on stock you don't hold.

Open If you purchase or write an option, creating a new position on that option, you establish an open position.

Open interest The number of contracts in existence in the market on a certain option.

Options chain A tool that lets you see all the available options for an underlying stock, including their prices and other trading data.

Options class All the calls or all the puts on an underlying security.

Options series All the calls or puts on an underlying stock with identical terms, including expiration month and strike price.

Out-of-the-money When a call's strike price is above the underlying stock price, or a put's strike price is below the stock price.

Physical delivery An option that calls for you to deliver if you're the writer, or receive if you're the holder, 100 shares of stock at exercise.

Premium The price you pay if you're an options buyer, or the amount you receive if you're an options writer.

Protective put You purchase a put on stock you already own.

Put If you buy a put, you hold the right to sell a certain number of shares at the strike price, on or before the expiration date. If you write a put, you face an obligation to buy a certain number of shares at the strike price, on or before the expiration date, if the put is exercised.

Put/call ratio A ratio of the number of puts traded compared to the number of calls traded for a particular options class.

Rolling Extending your options strategy by closing an existing position and opening a new one on the same underlying instrument with a different expiration or strike price.

Seller If you sell an option, whether opening a new position or closing an existing position, you're a seller.

Short When you have written an option. You may hold a short position, or be short.

Specialist A trader who leads the auction for an options class or a set of underlying securities, and maintains a fair and orderly market.

Spread An options strategy that calls for you to hold two or more simultaneous positions. Spread may also refer to the difference between an option's bid-ask price.

Stop-loss order An order you place to purchase an option or security that comes with an order to sell if the price drops below a certain limit in the future, or rises, if you've sold an option.

Strike price The price at which you may buy the underlying stock, if you hold a call, or sell the underlying stock, if you hold a put.

Terms The characteristics of your option, including strike price, exercise style, and expiration date.

Time decay The decline in value of your option as the expiration date approaches.

Time value The perceived and often-changing value of the time left until an option's expiration.

Vertical spread You simultaneously purchase and write two or more options with different strike prices and the same expiration month.

VIX The Volatility Index, or a compilation of volatility of several S&P 500 options. You might use VIX as a benchmark for the market's perception of volatility.

Volatility How much an option price fluctuates. Historical volatility is a measure of past actual fluctuations. Implied volatility is a gauge of the market's prediction for its future fluctuation.

Volume The number of positions that are traded, or opened and closed, during a time period for a specific option.

Wasting asset A security that loses value over time, and has no worth after a certain date.

Writer If you sell an option to open a new position, you're a writer.

INDEX

INDEX

INDEX